Supernatural

Testimonies

Compiled by

Commander Michael H. Imhof, U.S. Navy (ret.)

Evangel Press
Nappanee, IN

Special thanks to Patricia Plummer for administrative assistance and support. Unless otherwise identified, Scripture quotations are from the Authorized King James Version of the Bible.

Printed by Evangel Press
2000 Evangel Way
Nappanee, IN 46550
www.evangelpress.com

Printed in the United States of America

Imhof, Michael H.
    Supernatural Testimonies / by Michael H. Imhof
    p. cm.
    ISBN **1-933858-03-6**
    1.   2.   I.

Library of Congress Control Number 2006922312

"The Lord also will be a refuge for the oppressed,
a refuge in times of trouble.
And they that know thy name will put their trust in thee:
for thou, Lord, hast not forsaken them that seek thee."
Psalms 9:9-10

Jesus said,
"Verily, verily, I say unto thee,
Except a man be born again,
he cannot see the kingdom of God."
John 3:3

CONTENTS

FOREWORD

I was living in Afghanistan when the idea came to me about putting together a small book of supernatural testimonies. In reality, salvation through Jesus Christ is a supernatural event; however, I think you'll glean something special from each of these testimonies. Each has something to offer in its own special way, but ultimately, each testimony leads to the acceptance of Jesus Christ as Lord and Savior, the most important decision anyone can make in one's life. It should also be noted that permission was granted to use these testimonies.

Life brings with it the challenges of day-to-day living. There are many distractions and temptations which can lead to various problems and troubles if prudent decisions aren't made on a daily basis. The world has so many things to offer and tempt us with. Often, the choices seem appealing, but many of these choices lead to despair and hopelessness — that's because the world's system is not God's system. It leads people into chaotic and sinful ways if one is not careful. Sin appears fun for a season but its fruits lead to destruction.

The people in these testimonies came to realize that there was a void in their lives. What could fill that void? How could they get peace in their lives? As all Christians realize, that void is only filled by the saving grace of Jesus Christ. It doesn't mean, as Christians, that we still don't have to deal with the world and its inherent problems, but we have an advocate, Who will help us through. The path of the righteous grows brighter and brighter as the Book of Proverbs tells us. Christians have a wonderful future, and the sooner one gets started on the Christian path, the better. Blessings to all who read these testimonies. May they be a source of encouragement and exhortation, and let it be known that Jesus Christ has a deep love for all of us! To Him be all glory!

Michael H. Imhof
Commander, U. S. Navy, (ret.)

INTRODUCTION

The testimonies that you're about to read cover a broad spectrum of different lifestyles, as well as events that led unto salvation for the majority of these people. The Holy Spirit moves on us in different ways to draw us unto Him. Why God moves in one way for one person, and another way for another is in His divine providence. I know this: regardless of the way God moves on our hearts, it's all with the best intentions for our good.

So many times people look back over their lives and realize that God was tugging on their hearts all the time, but they wouldn't listen. Thus, people go their ways, make poor decisions and plunge into sin. As a result, people often call out to God in desperate situations. He's still there, and He still loves people. As a matter-of-fact, He wants to deliver us more than we want to be delivered. He wants to save us more than we want to be saved. God has such an awesome love for all of us, that we in the truest of terms, cannot truly fathom the depths of it.

As you read the personal testimonies of these people, perceive the love of God in their lives. Perceive how much God wanted to bring peace to their despondent situations. It's no different with you or I. There's not one reading this book that God does not want to reach out to. For a Christian, He wants to encourage you more in your walk with Him. For those in desperate situations, He wants to deliver you. For a non-believer, He wants to bring you unto salvation. Jesus Christ is your answer for any situation in this life, or the next, and let me say that no situation is too difficult for Him. Trust in the Lord.

CHAPTER 1

A Touch Of Lazarus
The John Wilson Story (as shared by son Terry Wilson)

Very few people die and come back to life. My dad, John Wilson, was one of those few ...

It was October 1987 when I returned to Melbourne, Australia from Darwin with my wife and boys. It was unusually warm for the spring of that year. It was like the sub-tropical weather warmed to greet us as we came down from the hot and sultry tropical Northern Territory. My family had not seen us for about three years, and they were in for a *big* surprise when they came face to face with the 'New Vessels' whom Christ Jesus had created!

My father had been suffering with emphysema for a number of years, owing to his work in concrete dust and his years working in steel foundries. His persistent smoking of cigarettes from a young age couldn't have helped him much either. His doctors didn't give him many months to live. I knew in my heart that God wanted me to share the gospel with him and to tell him that he needed Jesus in his life; so I took the step and told both my parents that they needed to be born again to enter into the Kingdom of God. Within the first ten minutes after sharing the gospel with them, I was told to get out because the Good News made them feel threatened for some reason. They may have even felt I was "on something," or that I was involved in some "scam or another," and was trying to pull them into it as well.

I went before the Lord about this problem and the Holy Spirit brought to mind that I should persist until the Lord told me to stop. For 12 months, I went to the house of my father to share the gospel with him, and each time he did not want to hear. Each day, he would put up with me sharing the Word, then send me on my way. At the end of the twelfth month I went before the Lord and cried out to Him that I was obedient to Him, yet I was at my wit's end! There seemed to be no receptiveness on my dad's part to hearing the truth that Jesus Christ paid the penalty for his sins by shedding His innocent blood on the Cross. My heart was so grieved...

At six-thirty the following morning I received a frantic phone call from my mother; my father had collapsed on the floor and was turning gray. She was so frantic that I had to organize the ambulance for her. The house we lived in at the time was on the same street as the local hospital. After organizing the ambulance, my wife and I ran up to the hospital. The ambulance arrived at the same time we did. I saw my mother get out of the ambulance, followed by my father on a gurney. As I looked at him, I saw the gray pallor of his face, and I knew what that meant. Pain so gripped my heart.

We entered the small cubical where my father had been placed. He was hooked up to an ECG machine, along with oxygen. As my mother, wife and myself stood over him, his heart stopped and the ECG signaled no heart beat. At that time I saw a 'black shadow' enshroud him. It seemed to come from the side of him and cover him. I was the only one to see this. He was dead.

Immediately, my mother cried out to me: "You are a *believer*, you can pray!" So for the benefit of my mother, I laid hands upon my father's body to thank the Lord for his life. What else could I do? He had resisted the gospel truth while he was alive. It was now time for him to answer to God. Suddenly, the Holy Spirit impressed upon me to begin to praise the Name of Jesus right then and there in that cubicle with doctors and nurses running everywhere! Joanne, my precious wife, joined me in praising the Lord.

People around probably thought that we were a bunch of nutcases. In the natural sense we were, but if you know what pleases God and creates an atmosphere for Him to work miracles down here ... well ... that's of another dimension. As we began our praises, that shadow lifted from my father's body and life returned to his body. Then I remembered the verse in Psalm 23: "Yea, though I walk through the valley of the shadow of death, I will fear no evil." Doctors ran in and out of the cubicle in frenzy bringing other doctors with them. They were truly bewildered over what had just happened.

My father opened his eyes and looked at me and I smiled at him, asking: "Are you ready to give your heart to Jesus *now?*" He said, "Yes!" I later found out that after we had left, the doctors gathered about him and told him that he had died. My father looked at them and told them that he had seen Jesus!

Not long after my father was discharged from the hospital, he became a real powerhouse for Jesus. Anyone who came through the door was told about Jesus. My other three brothers stayed well away. In fact, they accused Joanne and I of brainwashing him, rather than to accept the plain truth. He was "brainwashed" alright — brainwashed with the shed *blood* of Jesus!

Ten months later, I was spending time with God, and He laid it upon my heart that He was going to take my father home. I asked, "How long, Lord?" And he told me, "Two weeks." In the second week of that two-week period, he developed chest infections that caused him to be hospitalized. He knew that his time was up, and I told him what the Lord had spoken to my heart.

During those last days, we were able to prepare him for what was about to come, and a great peace was upon him. He was allowed to come home to spend his last days and we all took turns being with him. He passed away on my watch.

I write this testimony on behalf of my father because it was his desire that his story would be shared with those who would hear and I promised him that I would keep his testimony alive. You're a witness to his last will and spiritual testament.

Kind permission was given by Precious Testimonies to share this testimony.

2

CHAPTER 2

Make Yourself Ready
The Richard Madison Story

Is there *REALLY* a God? Maybe you have asked yourself that question many times, yet still are not sure. Or perhaps you have chosen to believe there *must* be a God, but just aren't sure what to believe about Him. Possibly you've read a variety of literature about what others believe about God, but about all that it has done is to trigger more questions. Which religion is right? Which is wrong? Are all right for those who believe they are right? Or, is a personal, intimate relationship with Jesus Christ the issue to focus on? Questions abound, don't they, about God, and the things of God?

So, what am I going to share about God that you probably don't already know? I'm going to tell you how I *experienced* God. Perhaps as I do so, your desire will increase to experience God as well.

Like many others, my childhood had its challenges. For instance, at six months old, I rolled off a couch and laid in a coma for six days. Then at age five, one of my great-uncles lost his mind and shot at me several times. I ran into my grandmother's house and hid under the bed. He shot my grandmother four times and later committed suicide. My grandmother lived though, and she credits it to the healing power of God.

At age 12, I gave my heart to Jesus Christ, and was water baptized at the local rock quarry. But as I grew older, I forgot about the Lord, and went my separate way. God simply calls it rebellion. Not surprisingly, I got into alcohol, drugs, and just plain riotous living. For 10 years, I ignored what the Bible has to say about the consequences that will come for people like me who believe on the Lord Jesus Christ, but make no effort to keep His commandments. As parents must discipline rebellious children for their own good, God also disciplines His rebellious spiritual children. "And ye have forgotten the exhortation which speaketh unto you as unto children, My son, despise not thou the chastening of the Lord, nor faint when thou art rebuked of him: For whom the Lord loveth he chasteneth, and scourgeth every son whom he receiveth. If ye endure chastening, God dealeth with you as with sons; for what son is he whom the father chasteneth not? But if ye be without chastisement, whereof all are partakers, then are ye bastards, and not sons. Furthermore we have had fathers of our flesh which corrected *us*, and we gave *them* reverence: shall we not much rather be in subjection unto the Father of spirits, and live? For they verily for a few days chastened *us* after their own pleasure; but he for *our* profit, that we might be partakers of his holiness. Now no chastening for the present seemeth to be joyous, but grievous: nevertheless afterward it yieldeth the peaceable fruit of righteousness unto them which are exercised thereby." (Hebrews 12:5-11).

During those rebellious years, there were times when I faced great peril, and I would call out on Jesus to come to my rescue, and He would. But when I wasn't in trouble, I'd forget about Him.

However, on April 13, 1986, at 6:45 a.m., I was unable to call upon Him. I was involved in a head-on collision. I went to sleep at the wheel and crossed the centerline. My 1984 Ford truck struck a 1985 Delta 88 head on. The engine of my truck was pushed into the cab, pushing my left leg up through my hip and pelvis. My right leg was pinned in under the dash, crushing my right ankle. The steering wheel crushed my chest, breaking all my ribs in front. One rib went into my right lung. Another rib cut the aorta artery in my heart. My spleen was ruptured. My left jaw was broken along with a vertebra in my neck. My right eye was knocked out of its socket. I was in bad need of a band-aid or two. Forty minutes passed before I was removed from the wreckage and transported to Vanderbilt University Hospital in Nashville, Tennessee.

I was considered dead on arrival, but the main trauma doctor later told me a voice from out of nowhere told him to try and save me. My aorta artery was repaired twice; my spleen was removed. I was considered brain dead since I had no blood carrying oxygen to my brain for 40 minutes. I was given a total of 124 units of blood.

To give the doctors a greater challenge, I got double pneumonia, blood poisoning, yellow jaundice, and hepatitis. My left hip, right ankle and left jaw remained broken for 25 days. Doctors felt it was useless to repair my bones when I was not going to survive anyway.

As I lay there in that hospital bed, teetering on the brink of death, three Christian believers in my family anointed me with oil and prayed the prayer of faith over me, believing God to heal me, in accordance with James 5:14-16 in the Bible. ("Is any sick among you? let him call for the elders of the church; and let them pray over him, anointing him with oil in the name of the Lord: And the prayer of faith shall save the sick, and the Lord shall raise him up; and if he have committed sins, they shall be forgiven him. Confess *your* faults one to another, and pray one for another, that ye may be healed. The effectual fervent prayer of a righteous man availeth much.")

On day 27 of my comatose state, my liver and kidneys stopped working. I laid in this condition with infections, swelling, and a fever of 104 degrees for 10 hours. The doctors called all of the family in one last time and advised them to make funeral arrangements. But the three determined Christians whom the Holy Spirit had given faith, stood on this promise: "Jesus said unto him, If thou canst believe, all things are possible to him that believeth." (Mark 9:23).

Members of my family went to the prayer chapel. While they were praying, I either had a vision, or my spirit left my body. I saw myself leave the Intensive Care Unit and walk down a hallway. I entered a door, realizing I was

4

in some sort of a church. I saw my family praying. I heard my name mentioned. I saw the color of the carpet and counted the number of the pews. While watching my family pray for me, I spoke to my mother, but she could not hear me. This was the end of my life... it seemed.

Then I had this *knowing* that I was not walking in right relationship with Jesus Christ, nor had I been in nearly 10 years. Was Jesus giving me one last chance to call on His Name? Suddenly I looked up and called on the Name of Jesus. All of a sudden, I felt a huge hand cover the top of my head. A voice said: "I am Jesus. I am giving you another chance. Go and tell my people I am the same yesterday, today, and forever, and I change not. Tell them I still perform miracles, and I am coming SOON."

I tried to look up at Him but He would not let my head turn. As I pushed against His hand, I sat up out of the 27-day coma. I reached for the nurse at the foot of the bed. I had a tracheotomy and my jaw was wired shut, so I wrote on paper the color of the carpet and the number of pews in the church. The nurse realized I was describing the prayer chapel and hurried down and found my family praying. She told them I was awake and okay, and that they must be praying to the REAL God.

After five days without medicine, the main trauma doctor came in my room and told me that he had never seen anything like what had happened to me. He said there must be a God in heaven, and He was watching over me.

I left the hospital in a wheelchair and was told that I would never walk again. The sciatic nerve was severed and three bones were removed in my right foot. But after eight weeks from the time of leaving the hospital, Jesus spoke to me and told me to arise and walk. I knew I was delivered from drugs and alcohol and even virtually raised from the dead, but to walk on legs I could not feel? My mind said it was impossible! But Jesus told me that I must begin to walk by faith, not by feelings. ("For we walk by faith, not by sight." 2 Corinthians 5:7).

Little did I realize at the time that He was teaching me one of the most important foundations in the Christian walk, not to mention how to see miracles manifest. I stood up out of the wheelchair and leaned forward. There was no feeling in my legs. Then I began to run. My legs just began to operate! I gave up the wheelchair for a walker. A week later, I traded that for a cane. A week later, I didn't need anything, and I've been walking with Jesus Christ ever since!

The Lord gave me a wonderful wife in 1988. In 1992, she saved my life by donating to me one of her kidneys. For a living, non-related donor to match the blood and tissue type of another person is almost impossible. We believed that Jesus was healing my kidneys and/or my body would accept Laura's kidney since we had become one flesh. I prayed for many kidney patients while I was on dialysis for nine weeks and many were healed. The Lord told me that many were the afflictions of the righteous, but He would deliver us out of them all.

5

The transplant was very successful, and the kidney began to work immediately. Laura and I left the hospital 8 days after the surgery, and I was preaching 15 days after the transplant. I have never had any type of rejection. This was truly a miracle.

Read the book, *Raised From The Dead* by Richard Madison or contact him at www.rickmadison.org.

So dear reader, if you want to *experience* God for yourself, don't let this moment pass without making Jesus Christ your Savior and Lord. But you must be serious about it. You must be willing to give your all to Him and be obedient to His commandments in the New Testament. When you do that, you'll have a glorious *experience* of your own to share, and it will be ONGOING! This age as we know it is winding down, and when Christ comes back for those who are sold out to Him, which He told me is *SOON,* we will forever be in the presence of God. No more prison, no more sadness, sickness or sorrow. Just pleasure forevermore!

CHAPTER 3

The Night Jesus Came To Visit
The Abby B. Conley Story

I was either five or six years old (I can't remember for sure). I shared a bedroom with my little sister at the time. I had been sleeping. When I awoke, I was sitting straight up in my bed. There stood Jesus Christ, just above my sister's bed (her bed was right next to mine). A peace came over my young body. Although I never met Him before, I immediately knew it was Jesus! He did not speak to me out of His mouth. He spoke His thoughts into my mind. He simply told me not to argue with my sister. My thoughts raced; I wanted to explain why I argued with my sister. Jesus knew what I was thinking. Before I could utter a word, my thoughts were seized, and a knowing came over me. I simply was being told, and I did not need to provide Him with an explanation. I don't remember Him leaving, nor going back to sleep. This entire interaction lasted five seconds. The next day when I awoke, and for months after that, I could not stop thinking about His visit.

As my life unfolded my parents abandoned me after years of emotional, mental and physical abuse. At the age of 12 my parents paid to have me live in a Girls Ranch for seven months. The program leadership did not feel that I belonged there, and released me back to my parents. My parents told me to leave and never come back, within weeks after I returned home. I then became a child of the streets in Phoenix, Arizona. Many bad things happened to me during this time in my life. I had no home, no money, food was hard to come by, and I remember not wanting to live during most of those long years. My parents had thrown me away, like trash. They simply could not be bothered with a child they did not want. My spirit broke.

When I was 16 years old, the Phoenix court system had heard about my situation, and I became a ward of the court. I was placed into a foster home until I was 18 years old. I would grow to an adult, still broken. I abused drugs, and alcohol. I tried very hard to take my life on two occasions.

I learned some things about Jesus Christ in the five seconds I spent with Him as a child. As I grew even older, I often meditated on that visit. It turned out to be what fixed the brokenness. Here is what I learned:

- *Jesus Christ knew what was going to happen to me, years before it happened.*
- *Even if we do not have parents in this world, we have a Father in heaven.*
- *He cares about us, even when no one else does.*
- *He knows what we think, and what is in our heart.*
- *He can communicate to us, without speaking.*
- *Although He came to me first, it took me coming to Him before I could start living life in the light.*

- *Jesus had wisdom about not arguing with my sister. I know that her lifestyle today has everything to do with the abuse that she suffered as a child at the hands of our parents. In many ways my sister suffered a worse fate. She lived with abusive parents, until she was a young adult. The short time she and I would share together should not have been wasted in quarrels.*
- *I was blessed to be thrown away, because Jesus caught me.*
- *Jesus had long brown wavy hair. He had a white robe on, and He stood in the air with confidence and ease (much like we stand on earth or solid ground). I am 42 years old as I type these words, I have never seen anyone in our world with that ability besides Him.*

Psalms 27:10 states, "When my father and mother forsake me, then the Lord will take me up."

CHAPTER 4

Marine For Jesus
The Jim Baxter Story

My brother and I joined the U.S. Marine Corps right out of high school and went away to World War II. Our mother, a true believer, wrapped us in Psalm 91 and claimed God's promises over us. My brother went to the Paramarine/Raiders and the Fifth Marine Division, and I went to the Office of Strategic Services and the Second Marine Division. We both went through combat and returned home safely after the war.

In 1950, with the outbreak of the Korean War, we were both recalled to active duty with the First Marine Division. Our mother again wrapped us in Psalm 91, gave each of us a small New Testament, and again sent us off to war with the Lord's blessing.

As a 12-year old, I had accepted the Lord but had never been well-disciplined or obedient. I wanted to play patty-cake in the sand piles of the world. At 25, when I went to Korea, I started reading the little New Testament my mother had given me.

At the Inchon landing, and for the next two weeks of heavy combat as a rifle squad leader, I read a few Bible verses every day. I loved my brother Marines who suffered and died alongside me. As the death and destruction grew more intense — and as I stood on the brink of eternity — I did not like what I saw.

As my outfit, Fox Company [F-2-1], attacked up the streets of Seoul, I was hit with a machine-gun bullet. I made it behind a burning police sub-station in the middle of the street. My corpsman, Chico, dressed my wounds and as sniper bullets crashed into the street beside us, he laid on top of me — covering me with his own body — and yelled in my ear, "You've had enough!" Other riflemen nailed the snipers and as Chico left me to help other Marines lying wounded in the street, he was hit by two bullets that blew the shinbone out of his leg. I never saw Chico again.

Several Marines threw a wooden door on the ground, rolled me on it and ran me down the street under heavy fire. It was a fearsome ride. I was given a shot of morphine, and dreamed during a beautiful, restful sleep to Kimpo airfield and the flight to Japan.

At Yokosuka Naval Hospital for three months, I proclaimed my loyalty to Chico, my corpsman. One night, the Lord came to me. I saw the blood running down His forehead, into His eyes, and down over His cheeks. I looked into His blood-filled eyes. He spread out His bloody hands and said, "*I did this for you.*"

I was willing to be loyal to Chico, but had not been willing to be loyal to the Lord. The Lord said, "*Come and follow me. I will make you a man. Put*

9

away childish things." I knew what he meant. I said, "Yes Sir."

With the Lord as the Lord of my life, I rejoined my outfit and went back into front-line combat for another five months before returning home.

My brother came home with frostbitten feet and I came home with a tender rear-end. Our mother cried with joy unspeakable. We were both baptized and have been His loyal Marines ever since. Everyday we say, "Yes Sir," to the Lord Jesus — our Champion and Hero, my Lord and my God.

I still pray for and bless Chico Carsonaro.

Kind permission was given by Precious Testimonies to share this testimony.

CHAPTER 5

Colin's Testimony
The Colin Anderson Story

I had been reading an old book about the Grape cure which tells you to eat only grapes for a month. In the book was a description of a neck collar which you put on and then hang yourself with it. The collar stretches your spine and makes you really healthy and taller. I thought I'd just use a rope instead and stretch my neck and spine that way. I got a rope and put it around my neck and carefully stepped off the chair so that the rope wouldn't jerk and break my neck. As soon as my weight was on the rope I saw a bright light above me and I felt pure love coming from the light. I had never felt so happy and I could feel myself leaving my body and moving into the light. Memories of my life passed before me and I knew I had died but I wasn't afraid. I just wanted to be free forever and I let myself float upwards into the light. It felt completely calm and serene and I thought about how everyone I knew would miss me, but I knew I was going to a better place.

Then I started to hear rustling and clicking sounds next to me and I turned around and saw Satan standing right next to me. He was wearing a red and black robe and his face looked like a living skeleton. I was terrified and I tried to get away, but I couldn't move. He put his face right next to mine and said he had been waiting for me and I had to go with him. I looked around for the loving light but it was gone and all I could see were ugly little creatures laughing at me. They looked like trolls or goblins.

Then I felt myself being grabbed from behind and held tightly and then I was raped by these demons. I started to scream and cry out to God to help me, and all the small devils laughed in small cackling voices; and then suddenly everything stopped and I felt myself falling very fast back into my body. My friend was calling my name and holding my body up while she took the noose off my neck. I was twitching violently and couldn't control myself. She lay me on the floor and after a few minutes I regained control of myself. I didn't tell her what had happened because I knew she wouldn't believe me. I went and bought a Bible that day and sat in the church reading it and praying for God to save me from Satan. I was 17 when that happened and when I was 33 Satan appeared again in my house.

Further, when I was a small boy I was taken to hell. I was made to watch big guards with spears herding people before a magistrate who was sitting on a throne. One by one the people stood in front of the magistrate and he read out their crimes from a scroll. Then the guards took hold of the person and threw them off the cliff into the fiery lake. There were lots of people in the lake and they didn't die, they just writhed around in agony. They held up their arms and their flesh was dripping off them. Many years later I saw an oil painting of the exact same hell. Everything was the same in every detail. It was obvious that someone else had seen the same hell I had seen, so I knew it was not just me.

Once when I was about 19, I was riding my bike past an old cemetery, and above the wall I saw a stone angel reaching up to God. I thought it looked beautiful so I went in to get a closer look. The angel was about five or six feet tall and was standing on top of a thick stone pillar. When I got to the angel's feet I looked up and suddenly the sky seemed to open and a heavenly light poured down onto me. I could feel the love of my heavenly Father soaking into every atom of my being and my heart melted with pure love for Him. I remembered that He was my greatest friend and somehow I had forgotten Him. I wept bitterly for hours and the light kept pouring onto me the whole time. Eventually, I went home and was a completely changed person.

CHAPTER 6

Marriage On The Only Rock
The Judy Rousseau Story

On my husband's 40th birthday, he turned to me and said, *"Judy, I need to tell you something; I just don't love you anymore."* I could hardly believe what I was hearing. At that time, we'd been married about 22 years. Things weren't great but I didn't think they were that bad. In the months that followed, our relationship deteriorated to the point that our home was filled with tension and strife. Our four children were getting pretty stressed, too. There was a lot of fighting, yelling and slamming doors. It reached the point that I finally asked my husband to move out.

Paul moved in with a friend of his. We were both hurting. I thought I was right and he thought he was right. At the time, it seemed more important to be justified in our anger than it did to try to work things out. Surely I didn't deserve to be treated so poorly after all I've done for him. *(I hope you can detect the self-righteous attitude, because believe me, I certainly had one.)*

There wasn't much communication going on. We both worked full-time and were now living about 40 minutes away from each other. Neither of us had anything good to say so we simply said nothing. My husband wasn't getting any positive attention from me and became vulnerable to the affections of a very attractive divorced woman that he worked with. When I learned about the affair, I decided that the only thing for me to do was to get a lawyer to draw up divorce papers. I gave my lawyer all the necessary information and couldn't wait until she would *just* "get this thing over with." For some reason, I thought a divorce was the answer or at least what was expected of me under the circumstances. The weeks went on and the lawyer seemed to be dragging her feet. Eventually she told me, "Judy, I have to be honest with you. I walk with God; and, because I do ... I can not proceed with your case. I will not be party to burying something that isn't dead. I believe if you will be patient, your marriage can be saved."

Never have I felt such despair. What would I do now? I had no lawyer and I certainly didn't want to go through providing all that information to someone else. I have to admit, the time that I was pursuing a divorce were some of the blackest, most hopeless days I've ever lived. I had no peace.

I sought help from a beloved Christian friend who had known me for some time. She asked me, "Judy, if God were standing right in front of you and asked you what you would like Him to do for you ... what would you tell Him?" The words came easily as my eyes filled with tears. I said, "I would ask Him to bring my husband back to Himself and back to our family. I would ask Him to use our family as an example of His ability to heal and restore."

My friend, Jeanne said, "Well then, we know how to pray ... don't we?"

All of a sudden, everything seemed so simple. Within a few days God spoke to me and said, *"Yes, Judy. You do have grounds for divorce and I will permit it if that is what you want. However, if you are willing to walk with me through this time, I will bring you great victory. But ... it will be very difficult."*

At that moment, I chose to allow the Lord to bring me the great victory He promised. At first, I expected that my husband would be home any day. I thought God was going to hit him with a "lightning bolt" and correct everything that was wrong in his life. Boy, was I wrong. God began to change me. He taught me so much as I waited on him. God allowed me to see that the love that I had for my husband was not really love at all. He showed me that. He loved me in spite of my imperfections, unconditionally. Could I offer my husband any less? God's truth and mercy exposed my selfishness and I sought His forgiveness. I contacted my husband to tell him the "great news" that I wanted to get back together with him. He was not impressed and told me that nothing had changed. He still did not love me and right now he was caught up in an exciting new romance.

As I waited on the Lord to bring me the great victory He promised, I began to be able to identify with His suffering and the rejection He had felt. Yet, He chose to love anyway. He did not throw stones at the adulterous woman; He offered her mercy and forgiveness and as His follower, I needed to treat my husband the same way.

People thought I was crazy. Why in the world would I hold on to someone who was treating me so? Certainly, God does not expect me to suffer in this way. Even Christians counseled me to get a divorce, saying God had someone better for me. Over and over again, God gave me the grace to put more faith in His word than the words of other people. Three of my four children didn't understand why I was holding on to their father and praying for him. My son, Mark, who loves the Lord and walks with Him, was given a vision that someday his dad would be back. He was a constant source of encouragement to me. My other children focused on the pain that we were all going through. It was stressful being a single parent, having to be both Mom and Dad, work full-time and take care of the house, etc.

As I was burdened down with single parenthood, my husband was living the life of a free man with no cares and no commitment. He would spend most of his time with his girlfriend and her three children and whenever he wanted to take off for a ride on his motorcycle, he was gone. Paul had become very bitter about the things of God and said to me. "I bet you think that GOD is going to do some great big miracle in my life ... don't you?" I did not answer, but in my heart I said ... *"YES!!!"*

I prayed for my husband a lot — probably at least two hours throughout the course of each day. I searched the Scriptures and underlined hundreds of promises God wrote to encourage and guide me. He also raised up several

14

faithful prayer partners to encourage me and keep me accountable to the decision I had made. I could probably write an entire book about these wonderful individuals, but I don't want to distract you from the story of my marital miracle-in-process.

However, there is one prayer partnership that I really need to tell you about because it is such an awesome story. One day, my two youngest boys and I were headed to Wal-Mart. For some strange reason that I didn't know at the time, I chose to go through the center of Milford, New Hampshire rather than take the bypass. There in the center of the Milford oval was a traffic rotary which was completely bottlenecked — no one was moving. I casually looked to my left and saw a motorcycle headed in the opposite direction only a couple of feet away from my car. I was stunned; it was my husband with his girlfriend's arms tightly wrapped about him. Out of impulse, I tooted the horn and waved. He dropped his sunglasses and sheepishly waved to me and within seconds the traffic moved him along the highway and he was gone.

I took a deep breath and told my boys that they needed to help me pray. (I'm sure they rolled their eyes thinking that their mom was crazy.) I began to pray a prayer something like this: *"Lord, what just happened here has to be something that You arranged because even if I tried to meet Paul at this precise spot at this precise time, something would have gone wrong. There is absolutely no reason for Paul to be here right now. He usually works Saturdays, he lives almost an hour away, and the timing of this meeting today is too perfect for it to be anything other than a miracle. Of all the millions of people in this world, who aren't my husband, You put him right there at the exact moment when I could not miss seeing him. Lord, Your Word says that You will work all things together for good because I love You and am called according to Your plan; so Father, I ask You to work good even from this difficult situation. Take hold of my heart and make me the person You desire me to be. Encourage my sons to trust You that You will one day bring their father home. For all these things I praise you in Jesus' Name. Amen."*

When I arrived at Wal-Mart, I heard the Lord speak to me once again. He said, *"Judy, today I am going to raise up someone in Wal-Mart who is going to pray for you and your family."* Hmmm... I wonder who, I thought as I locked up the car. I gave my boys their instructions and asked them to meet me in an hour in front of the checkout. I then began to question the Lord about how I would know the person. He responded, "You will know."

I stood still for about a minute and one-half in front of the Lawn and Garden Department and then a young man passed by. His shirt read, "The Lord's gym — His pain, your gain." As the man walked by, the Lord said, *"That is the man."* I followed him, beginning to rehearse what I would say to him, and found him kneeling down looking at fishing equipment in the sports section of the store.

I uttered a silent prayer, took a deep breath and tapped him on the shoulder. "Excuse me," I said. "I've never done anything like this before, but today as I got out of my car here at Wal-Mart, the Lord spoke to me. He said that He was going to raise up someone in Wal-Mart who was going to pray for me and my family. When you walked by, the Lord told me that person is you." The man jumped to his feet raised his hands in the air and said, "Praise the Lord". *"Yes,"* I thought… *" this is the right guy."* Can you imagine what would have happened if I'd picked the wrong person. Security probably would have put me on permanent lay-away!

The man asked how he could pray for me. I now introduced myself and told him that my boys and I had just seen my husband on his motorcycle with his girlfriend, but that I believed God to restore him to Himself, and then back to me and our children.

The anointing of God came over this wonderful brother and he spoke, "Judy, you keep your eyes firmly planted on the Word of God. Don't look to the left, don't look to the right, don't listen to man, don't listen to woman; but keep your eyes firmly planted on the Word of God. For I want to tell you, Judy, your husband's relationship with this other woman CANNOT and *WILL NOT* PREVAIL AGAINST THE WORD AND WILL OF ALMIGHTY GOD!!!!

Wow!!! I was so overwhelmed I nearly fell over backwards. I felt as if I was face to face with an Old Testament prophet. The words he spoke ministered such hope to me that I thought on them many times during the remaining days of our separation. Several times the "prophet's" words reminded me not to heed the advice of well-meaning friends, but to focus only on the Word and Will of God.

After I recuperated from the impact of what he spoke, I asked him his name and a little bit about himself. He told me that his name was Adam and that he and his wife Dorothy lived nearby. He then allowed me to talk for a few more minutes giving him details and Paul's business card to remind him to pray.

After I had spilled out all that I had to say, this patient man said to me that he had something to tell me. He proceeded to tell me that he had been praying that the Lord would use his life to help others. Adam admitted to me that he had observed God's supernatural workings in the lives of his friends but had never really experienced such a move of God himself, so he had included a special request in his prayer that someday the Lord would touch his life in a supernatural way. He closed his prayer with a typical amen and then went into Wal-Mart to buy some fishing equipment.

Suddenly, this little lady whom he has never seen before, taps him on the shoulder and tells him that he is the one that God had chosen to help her pray for her family. So, when Adam jumped to his feet, he did so because that supernatural prayer of his had been answered.

Now some may say that my Wal-Mart story is a coincidence, but I think NOT. When I think about what happened that Saturday afternoon, I am powerfully moved by how God's hand knows exactly where everyone will be and at what precise moment. His hand arranged that I would see my husband and then that I would meet Adam (and he would meet me) at just the right moment. I ask you, what are the chances of this happening all by itself? I just love the way that God can answer the prayers of two strangers through the same set of circumstances.

I also received a lot of support from my pastor who offered me and my prayer partners the use of the church on Monday nights. We gathered every Monday night for prayer after fasting all day. This evolved into a Monday night prayer meeting for marriages and families, which continues to this day. Four to eight of us meet every week and pray for couples that have been brought to our attention.

Things began to change in Paul's life and he began to reach out to the Lord for help. He admits that his life had become such a mess, but I'm so grateful to say that after three and one-half years, my prodigal husband returned to the Lord and our family. It took a long time, but God has made a new man out of him and neither of us are the same people we once were. Our children rejoice as well and are now fully healed from the pain of that difficult time.

I pray that this testimony brings you hope, peace and encouragement. What God has done for us, He *can* and *will* do for you.

CHAPTER 7

The Birdies
This is a true story that occurred in 1994 and was told by Lloyd Glen.

On July 22nd, I was enroute to Washington, D.C. for a business trip. It was all so very ordinary, until we landed in Denver for a plane change. As I collected my belongings from the overhead bin, an announcement was made for Mr. Lloyd Glenn to see the United Customer Service Representative immediately. I thought nothing of it until I reached the door to leave the plane and I heard a gentleman asking every male if they were Mr. Glenn. At this point I knew something was wrong and my heart sunk. When I got off the plane, a solemn-faced young man came toward me and said, "Mr. Glenn, there is an emergency at your home. I do not know what the emergency is, or who is involved, but I will take you to the phone so you can call the hospital." My heart was now pounding, but the will to be calm took over.

Woodenly, I followed this stranger to the distant telephone where I called the number he gave me for the Mission Hospital. My call was put through to the Trauma Center where I learned that my three-year old son had been trapped underneath the automatic garage door for several minutes, and that when my wife had found him, he was dead. CPR had been performed by a neighbor, who is a doctor, and the paramedics had continued the treatment as Brian was transported to the hospital.

By the time of my call, Brian was revived and they believed he would live, but they did not know how much damage had been done to his brain, nor to his heart. They explained that the door had completely closed on his little sternum, right over his heart. He had been severely crushed. After speaking with the medical staff, my wife sounded worried but not hysterical, and I took comfort in her calmness. The return flight seemed to last forever, but finally I arrived at the hospital, six hours after the garage door had come down. When I walked into the Intensive Care Unit, nothing could have prepared me to see my little son laying so still on a great big bed with tubes and monitors everywhere. He was on a respirator. I glanced at my wife who stood by his side — it was like a terrible dream. I was filled in with the details and given a guarded prognosis. Brian was going to live, and the preliminary tests indicated that his heart was okay — two miracles, in and of themselves. Only time would tell if his brain received any damage.

Throughout the seemingly endless hours, my wife was calm. She felt that Brian would eventually be all right. I hung on to her words and faith like a lifeline. All that night and the next day, Brian remained unconscious. It seemed like forever since I had left for my business trip the day before. Finally, at two o'clock that afternoon, our son regained consciousness and sat up uttering the most beautiful words I have ever heard spoken. He said, "Daddy, hold me", and he reached for me with his little arms.

By the next day he was pronounced as having no neurological or physical deficits and the story of his miraculous survival spread throughout the hospital. You cannot imagine our gratitude and joy.

As we took Brian home, we felt a unique reverence for the life and love of our Heavenly Father that comes to those who brush death so closely. In the days that followed, there was a special spirit about our home. Our two older children were much closer to their little brother. My wife and I were much closer to each other, and all of us were very close as a whole family. Life took on a less stressful pace. Perspective seemed to be more focused, and balance much easier to gain and maintain. We felt deeply blessed. Our gratitude was truly profound.

Almost a month later, to the day of the accident, Brian awoke from his afternoon nap and said, "Sit down, Mommy, I have something to tell you." At this time in his life, Brian usually spoke in small phrases, so to say a large sentence surprised my wife. She sat down with him on his bed and he began his sacred and remarkable story.

"Do you remember when I got stuck under the garage door? Well, it was so heavy and it hurt really bad. I called to you, but you couldn't hear me. I started to cry, but then it hurt too bad. And then the 'birdies' came."

"The birdies?" my wife asked, puzzled.

"Yes," he replied. "The 'birdies' made a whooshing sound and flew into the garage. They took care of me."

"They did?"

"Yes," he said. "One of the 'birdies' came and got you and she came to tell you I got stuck under the door."

A sweet reverent feeling filled the room. The spirit was so strong and yet lighter than air. My wife realized that a three-year old had no concept of death and spirits, so he was referring to the beings who came to him from beyond as 'birdies' because they were up in the air like birds that fly.

"What did the birdies look like?" she asked.

Brian answered. "They were so beautiful. They were dressed in white — all white. Some of them had green and white. But some of them had on just white."

"Did they say anything?"

"Yes," he answered. "They told me the baby would be all right."

"What baby?"

And Brian answered, "The baby laying on the garage floor." He went on, "You came out and opened the garage door and ran to the baby. You told the baby to stay and not leave."

My wife nearly collapsed upon hearing this, for she had indeed gone and knelt beside Brian's body. Seeing his crushed chest and unrecognizable features, knowing he was already dead, she looked up around her and whispered, "Don't leave us Brian, please stay if you can."

As she listened to Brian telling her the words she had spoken, she realized that the spirit had left his body and was looking down from above. "Then what happened?" she asked.

"We went on a trip, far, far away..." He grew agitated trying to say the things he didn't seem to have the words for. My wife tried to calm him and comfort him, and let him know it would be okay. He struggled with wanting to tell something that was obviously very important to him, but finding the words was difficult.

"We flew so fast up in the air. They're so pretty, Mommy." he added. "And there are lots and lots of 'birdies'." My wife was stunned. Into her mind the sweet comforting spirit enveloped her more soundly, but with an urgency she had never known before.

Brian went on to tell her that the 'birdies' had told him that he had to come back and tell everyone about the 'birdies'. He said they brought him back to the house, and that a big fire truck and an ambulance were there. A man was bringing the baby out on a white bed and he tried to tell the man the baby would be okay, but the man couldn't hear him. He said, "Birdies told him he had to go with the ambulance, but they would be near him." They were so pretty and peaceful, he didn't want to come back. And then the bright light came. He said the light was so bright and so warm and he loved the bright light so much. Someone was in the bright light and put their arms around him and told him, "I love you but you have to go back. You have to play baseball, and tell everyone about the birdies." Then the person in the bright light kissed him and waved bye-bye. Then whoosh, the big sound came and they went into the clouds.

The story went on for an hour. He told us, "the 'birdies' were always with us, but we don't see them because we look with our eyes and we don't hear them because we listen with our ears. But they are always there; you can only see them in here (and he put his hand over his heart). They whisper the things to help us do what is right because they love us so much." Brian continued, stating "I have a plan, Mommy. You have a plan. Daddy has a plan. Everyone has a plan. We must all live our plan and keep our promises. The 'birdies' help us to do that because they love us all so much."

In the weeks that followed, he often came to us and told all, or part of it, again and again. Always the story remained the same. The details were never changed or out of order. A few times he added further bits of information and clarified the message he had already delivered. It never ceased to amaze us how he could tell such detail and speak beyond his ability when he spoke of his 'birdies'.

Everywhere he went, he told complete strangers about the 'birdies'. No one ever looked at him strangely when he did this. Rather, they always get a profound softened look on their face and smile. Needless to say, we have not been the same ever since that day, and I pray we never will be.

Kind permission was given by www.aleroy.com to share this testimony.

CHAPTER 8

Saved From Hell
The Kenneth E. Hagin Story

The following is an excerpt of his experience as described in his book,
I Believe in Visions, by Reverend Kenneth E. Hagin.

My heart stopped beating. This numbness spread to my feet, my ankles,
my knees, my hips, my stomach, my heart – and I leaped out of my body.

I did not lose consciousness; I leaped out of my body like a diver would
leap off a diving board into a swimming pool. I knew I was outside my body. I
could see my family in the room, but I could not contact them.

I began to descend – down, down, into a pit, like you'd go down into a
well, cavern or cave. And I continued to descend. I went down feet first. I
could look up and see the lights of the earth. They finally faded away. Darkness
encompassed me round about – darkness that is blacker than any night man has
ever seen.

The farther down I went, the darker it became – and the hotter it became –
until finally, way down beneath me, I could see fingers of light playing on the
wall of darkness. And I came to the bottom of the pit.

This happened to me more than 60 years ago, yet it's just as real to me as
if it happened the week before last.

When I came to the bottom of the pit, I saw what caused the fingers of
light to play on the wall of darkness. Out in front of me, beyond the gates or
the entrance into hell, I saw giant, great orange flames with a white crest.

I was pulled toward hell just like a magnet pulls metal unto itself. I knew
that once I entered through those gates, I could not come back.

I was conscious of the fact that some kind of creature met me at the
bottom of the pit. I didn't look at it. My gaze was riveted on the gates, yet I
knew that a creature was there by my right side.

That creature, when I endeavored to slow down my descent, took me by
the arm to escort me in. When he did, away above the blackness and the
darkness a voice spoke. It sounded like a male voice, but I don't know what he
said. I don't know whether it was God, Jesus, an angel or who. He did not
speak in the English language: it was a foreign language.

That place just shook at the few words he spoke! And the creature took his
hand off my arm. There was a power like a suction to my back parts that pulled
me back. I floated away from the entrance to hell until I stood in the shadows.
Then, like a suction from above, I floated up, head first, through the darkness.

Before I got to the top, I could see the light. I've been down in a well: it
was like you were way down in a well and could see the light up above.

22

I came up on the porch of my grandpa's house. Then I went through the wall – not through the door, and not through the window – through the wall, and seemed to leap inside my body like a man would slip his foot inside his boot in the morning time.

Before I leaped inside my body, I could see my grandmother sitting on the edge of the bed holding me in her arms. When I got inside my body, I could communicate with her.

I felt myself slipping. I said, "Granny, I'm going again. You've been a second mother to me when Momma was ill."

My heart stopped for a second time. I leaped out of my body and began to descend: down, down, down. Oh, I know it was just a few seconds, but it seemed like an eternity.

There farther down I went, the hotter and darker it became, until I came again to the bottom of the pit and saw the entrance to hell, or the gates as I call it. I was conscious that that creature met me.

I endeavored to slow down my descent – it seemed like I was floating down – yet it seemed like there was a pull that pulled me downward. And that creature took me by the arm. When he did, that voice spoke again – a man's voice. It was a foreign language. I don't know what he said, but when he spoke, that whole place just shook. That creature took his hand off my arm.

It was like a suction to my back. I never turned around. I just came floating back into the shadows of darkness. And then I was pulled up, head first. I could see the lights of the earth above me before I came up out of the pit. The only difference this time was that I came up at the foot of the bed. For a second time I stood there. I could see my body lying there on the bed. I could see Grandma as she sat there holding me in her arms.

(Kenneth E. Hagin says goodbye to his family)

I left a word for each of them, and my heart stopped the third time.

I could feel the circulation as it cut off. Suddenly my toes went numb. Faster than you can snap your fingers, my toes, feet, ankles, knees, hips, stomach and heart went dead – and I leaped out of my body and began to descend.

Until this time, I thought, this is not happening to me. This is just a hallucination. It can't be real!

But then I thought, "This is the third time. I won't come back this time! I won't come back this time!" Darkness encompassed me round about, darker than any night man has ever seen. And in the darkness, I cried out, "God! I belong to the church! I've been baptized in water."

I waited for an answer, but there was no answer; only the echo of my own voice through the darkness. And the second time I cried a little louder, "God! I belong to the church! I've been baptized in water!"

I waited for an answer, but there was no answer; only the echo of my own voice as it echoed through the darkness.

I came again to the bottom of that pit. Again I could feel the heat as it beat me in the face. Again I approached the entrance, the gates into hell itself. That creature took me by the arm. I intended to put up a fight, if I could, to keep from going in. I only managed to slow down my descent just a little, and he took me by the arm.

Thank God that voice spoke. I don't know who it was – I didn't see anybody – I just heard the voice. I don't know what he said, but whatever he said, that place shook; it just trembled. And that creature took his hand off my arm.

It was just like there was a suction to my back parts. It pulled me back, away from the entrance to hell, until I stood in the shadows. Then it pulled me up head first.

As I was going up through the darkness, I began to pray. My spirit, the man who lives inside this physical body, is an eternal being, a spirit man. I began to pray, "O God! I come to You in the Name of the Lord Jesus Christ. I ask You to forgive me of my sins and to cleanse me from all sin."

I came up beside the bed. The difference between the three experiences was that I came up on the porch the first time; I came up at the foot of the bed the second time; and I came up right beside the bed the third time.

When I got inside my body, my physical voice picked up and continued my prayer right in the middle of the sentence. I was already praying out of my spirit.

Now, we didn't have all the automobiles in 1933 that we have today – that was in the Depression. But they tell me that between me and Momma praying so loud, traffic was lined up two blocks on either side of our house! They heard me praying from inside the house, and they heard my mother as she walked the porch praying at the top of her voice.

I looked at the clock and saw it was 20 minutes before 8 o'clock. That was the very hour I was born again due to the mercy of God through the prayers of my mother.

Kind permission was given by Kenneth Hagin Ministries to share this testimony.

CHAPTER 9

Washed White as Snow
Contributed by Becky Fischer
(from her Grandfather's taped testimony)

He'd come home drunk again, cursing and yelling. Six-year old James had seen him like that many times before, but this time it was different. Somehow his dad seemed angrier than usual, and he was just being plain mean. There weren't many places to hide in that two room wooden shack, so when his dad began hollering at his tiny, soft-spoken Cherokee mother, the child could see and hear everything.

There was no reasoning with the Indian man that night, and as he screamed unfounded accusations at his wife, he reached for the big, heavy iron rod that the family used for a fire poker. In a drunken stupor he wielded it through the air and connected with his wife's head. The little boy, already terrified at the scene, screamed in horror as the blood literally gushed from the woman's head. She laid helpless and seemingly dead on the bare, wooden floor before him. James' mother was the most precious thing in all the world to him, and at the sight of the blood, he threw himself across her body, fearing the worst, that she was dead.

"I hate you! I hate you! I hate you!" he screamed at his father, who didn't even seem to understand the seriousness of what he'd just done. Each time the little boy spoke the words, it came out with growing vengeance. Something happened inside of him at that moment. A bitterness and anger entered his heart that never left him. James vowed at that young age that he would live for only one thing — to get big enough to kill his own father for what he'd done to his mother.

By some divine miracle, Mary Elizabeth Pepper did not die, but her recovery was very slow. There was no such thing as blood transfusions in those days in the tiny town in Missouri. But upon her recovery, she understandably left the home to move in with one of her older sons. James, the youngest of ten children, seldom saw her again. But James' troubles were just beginning. He was in and out of trouble with the law, thrown in jail numerous times for stealing, but he was always let go because he was a minor. An older brother once said of him: "He was the meanest little kid I ever knew." Frequently picked on by other kids, he nearly sliced a guy's hand off one time to get him to leave him alone.

James never went past the eighth grade in school, and spent his days helping take care of the little tobacco farm, where he got all the tobacco and homemade wine he wanted — stolen behind his dad's back, of course. By the time he was seventeen, misery and hatred were his constant companions. The day came when hopelessness consumed him and he thought of little else but ending his own life. It wasn't a matter of *if*, but of *how*. He'd lost count of the times he'd wondered about a place he'd heard about called heaven: where it was totally peaceful; where everybody loved each other; and no one ever went without food. He questioned, "Could there really be such a place?" If there was, he pondered, *Why not end it all and get out of the miserable life and go there*. He wondered if there really was a Great Spirit and what he was like. He knew nothing about a god or religion except for the little bit that he'd seen as his father performed some types of Indian rituals out by a tree in the yard. He'd never been to a white man's church or read a white man's Bible.

It was in one of those pensive, desperate moments that he sat all alone in the wooden shack on a stool at the table. Laid out before him were his hunting knife, a shiny new revolver and some poison. Among all the other questions that ran through his mind, he was trying to decide which of these was the quickest and most painless ways to do away with himself, when suddenly...

As he looked up at the wall in front of him, there stood a man he had never seen before, clothed in pure white. Before James could open his mouth, the man held His finger up to His lips as though to say, "Don't say anything." Then He spoke, "I've come to answer your questions," and He motioned, "Follow me."

The last thing James remembered at that moment was that he was beginning to stand, when the walls of that two-room shack rolled back and the teenager found himself following the white-robed man into a garden. The man kneeled before a rock and began to pray. Within moments, soldiers appeared, grabbing the man and forcibly taking him away.

The young Indian boy continued to follow this stranger and watched as he was whipped and beaten mercilessly, then finally nailed to a wooden cross. James found himself at the foot of that cross weeping and sobbing as the blood flowed from the man's hands and feet. He looked up at this kind individual, and somehow inside himself, he knew that this stranger on the cross was the Son of God. Just like he sobbed when he was a little boy laying in a pool of his mother's blood, he looked helplessly up at this man and cried out, "Why did you let them do this to you?" From the cross, the dying man looked down at James and said, "For you!"

With that, suddenly James was back in the kitchen of the little shack, still weeping like a child. He sat for the longest time thinking about what he'd just seen and heard, when he realized that The Stranger was standing before him once again clothed in glowing white garments. When James looked at Him the man spoke: "Though your sins were as scarlet, they have been made white as snow." Then He disappeared.

In that moment it was like a thousand pounds were lifted off James' shoulder. Every ounce of the hatred and anger and bitterness that had been his constant companions for so long, instantly disappeared. He had never felt so free. He glanced down at the items sitting on the table before him, which included his cigarettes, alcohol and gambling cards. A voice behind him said, "I guess you won't be needing those things anymore." The voice was so real, James turned to see if his father had entered the room, but no one was there. Then he realized it was the voice of the man clothed in white. "No, I guess I won't," he said, and with that he threw the cigarettes, the cards, and the alcohol away and never touched them again!

James' life was forever changed that day! Even the old mules that he plowed with, knew it. It was in the days when farmers walked behind the plows, holding the wooden handles, and throwing the leather straps that guided the mules, over their shoulders and around their necks. Whenever the old plows would hit a stump or a big rock, the jolt would throw James over the plow and under the feet of the mules. For many years as he'd been farming, when that would happen, James would began to rant and cuss and come up screaming and beating the mules as if it was their fault.

The first time James plowed after his life changing experience, he ended up under the feet of the mules once again, and he could see their hides begin to quiver. They were poised for the usual beating, but James quietly stood to his feet, dusted himself off and said, "Well, praise God!" The two old mules literally turned their heads and looked at him as though in disbelief. Even the mules knew he was changed!

It wasn't until later when James received a Bible and then searched the Word, that he read about the very scenes he had walked through by vision himself. In utter amazement he read the story of the crucifixion of the Son of God. He had been there! It was then that he learned that the Stranger's name was Jesus — Jesus Christ, Son of the Living God!

Kind permission was given by Precious Testimonies to share this testimony.

CHAPTER 10

Jesus Save Me
The Carmie Summers Story

I was raised Catholic but stopped going to church in my teen years. I married when I was in my mid-thirties and quit working before the birth of my first child. Two years later we moved from New York to Illinois for my husband's new job. A year later, I gave birth to another child and shortly thereafter we built a large home. I never returned to work in an office but felt at that point in my life, I was working harder than ever before, always trying to do my best to make things perfect for my family. At age 40, I began wondering if putting forth so much effort into everyday living was worth it, since I was only going to grow old and die anyway. Looking for answers, I went to the library and brought home numerous books, all with a different viewpoint regarding the mysteries of life. I stared at the huge pile of books sitting on my kitchen table, and then grew frustrated, realizing I would probably be dead before coming to any conclusions. Wanting a deeper understanding about life, I decided to say a short prayer asking God for enlightenment.

The next night, I was busy preparing a bath for my baby. My husband was away on business and I wasn't even thinking about God or the answers to life, when suddenly I felt a powerful presence in the room with me. I became very frightened and that fear evoked a vivid recollection of a scene from the movie *Falling Down*. The story involved a man who grew increasingly frustrated with his life and others around him. He began dealing with people more aggressively, believing that he, in his own way, was helping others. The movie concluded with a scene in which the character suddenly becomes "aware," and with great surprise, he shouts: "I'M THE BAD GUY?"

Immediately after the memory of that movie scene, I was launched into another realm, where instantly I had what appeared to be a life review. It is difficult to explain how I was able to see so much of my life in the blink of an eye, other than to say I felt like a super high-speed computer — able to rapidly process vast amounts of information. Since I associated a life review with death, I thought I might be having a heart attack; but in reality, I wasn't sick and I wasn't dying. Although I deeply loved my family and knew they deeply loved me, I was not shown any of the love I had shared with them or with anyone else. I was only seeing how I was hurting others. So like the character in the movie, I suddenly thought, *What, I'm the bad guy?*

As the life review slowed to an end, I heard (through mental telepathy) a male voice speak in a calm manner. It was similar to a doctor gently cluing-in his patient about the consequences of not maintaining proper health care; or it

28

was similar to a teacher helping a student understand the consequences of skipping classes and homework assignments. He asked, "Do you understand what is happening to you?" I just had a life review and associated that with death and judgment, and so I said, "Yes." The second question was "Do you understand the consequences of your sins?" Because I only saw how I was hurting others, and believing this was God judging me, I accepted that I was going to hell and so I answered, "Yes." The last question was "Do you understand you will be eternally separated from your children?" I was astonished when I heard this because I often wondered whether or not we really reunite with loved ones after we die. Now that I knew the answer, I felt I was getting the worst sentence – never seeing my children ever again. I wanted more than anything to return to the worldly realm to be with them, but knew that wasn't going to happen; and so with great sadness I answered the question with a "yes."

God gave me some time to think. As soon as I officially accepted my fate, I started falling down a dark void. I was frantically trying to find something to grab hold of, but there wasn't anything there, and so I kept falling into deeper darkness. The pace at which I was dropping, gradually slowed, and eventually I came to a stop where I found myself suspended in the air — hovering over flames. I heard the sound of a soul from within the flames screaming out in torment — moaning and wailing. I was scared beyond belief, knowing that soon I would be in that same place. Horrified, I called out for help. I called for my mother, my husband and a neighbor, but no one was there to hear me. There was nothing, just silence. All I had was the pain of being separated from my family in a place so awful that it would be impossible to describe.

I was completely alone, and at that moment in time, realized how much we all depend upon one another and how I might have taken for granted the people who were there for me when I needed them. I wanted another chance to show just how much I appreciated everyone, so I prayed to God to give me that chance. As I prayed, I saw a tiny pinpoint of light piercing through the darkness, then another, then there were thousands of tiny points of light. They grew larger and larger and soon spelled out the words JESUS CHRIST. I looked at this huge display of blazing lights but was not sure what to make of it. I thought, *Jesus Christ? What does He have to do with anything; He was probably just a man anyway.* Suddenly an image came to mind – it was that of a sign that I would drive by each day on my way home. It said: *Are You Saved – Only Jesus Saves?* I thought about those words for a while and had a feeling they were important.

Since I always lived in predominantly Catholic neighborhoods in New York where it would be unusual to hear the expression "Are You Saved – Only Jesus Saves?", I did not understand what the question was asking. I only remembered being taught that Jesus died in order to open the gates of heaven for all of mankind. I struggled for a while and then slowly began to put words together like "Jesus......Savior." I thought, *Savior from what and for what?* Then the whole thing just hit me. *JESUS...SAVIOR...OH, MY!!! Maybe Jesus can save me!!!* ... And I screamed out "JESUS SAVE ME!!!!"

All of a sudden I was pulled up and out of the dark hole and into another realm where again I felt like a super high-speed computer being downloaded with all the answers about life. As this information passed into my being, I was amazed because the answers to some of life's most complex questions appeared quite simple. I saw years of biblical history pass before my eyes, including the crucifixion. I could hardly believe what I was seeing. I thought to myself, *Wow! This stuff really happened. Get me out of here — I have to go tell the world!!!!!* God communicated with me for the last time with this message: "Do you see how blind you were? That is how blind your family is. Now, go and save your family." Then — BOOM! I was right back in the room again, in the same spot with the towel in my hand.

Filled with emotion, I called my next door neighbor and tried to explain what happened. She immediately came over with a Bible and said, "I think you just got saved." Not knowing what "saved" meant, I didn't quite understand. Later my husband called to check in. I answered the phone in tears. He asked why I was so upset but I could barely speak and simply said I was sorry for hurting him. He said I hadn't done anything that he was hurting over. I said I was sorry for any time I had ever hurt him.

Over the course of the next few months, I read the Bible over and over again, mostly the New Testament. I had never read a Bible before that time and was astounded to find out that what I was reading in the Bible was exactly what I had seen when taken through biblical times. At that point I was absolutely certain Jesus was God.

CHAPTER 11

Where Shall I Hide
The Neavei Isaac Story

Neavei Isaac, the author, currently resides in Queensland, Australia. He was born and raised in New Zealand.

I want to tell you about the single most important event in my life. In doing so I will have to reveal some things of a personal nature. I guess almost everyone has things in their personal history which they would rather be otherwise. There is no profit in dwelling on things which have been cast into the sea of forgetfulness; they are recalled here only to provide some necessary background.

I was born in New Zealand. My mother rejected me for several days, claiming that I wasn't her child. Some days later she repented and took me home, where I was rejected by my dad. For the most part he ignored me, but that became more difficult as the months passed. Obviously, I don't remember much of that except that these things were sometimes mentioned as I grew up. I had a very difficult early childhood.

By the time I was school age my parents had become convinced that I was evil and stupid. Whenever I got into trouble, which was often, they would tell me how evil and stupid I was. Sometimes Dad would say that Mother should have given me away at birth. Throughout my upbringing I was treated differently from my brothers and sister. It was not until I was forty-eight years old that I discovered the reason for all this.

Before Dad died, he told my sister who later told me, that he believed I was not his son; he said that Mother had been raped, and I was the result.

The moment I heard that, many things that had puzzled me fell into place. Bits of overheard conversation and many bewildering comments from relatives all suddenly made perfect sense. Partly heard snatches of conversation...., and words like, "love-child, mamser, bastard" now had a context which made them understandable.

Once I understood the truth, I was able to have compassion for this man who had been presented with his wife's bastard child. I forgave him for all the bad things that happened between us, and was able to let go of a great deal of bitterness and resentment that I had been carrying around with me all my life. I want to honor my parents for doing the best they could in a very difficult situation. They were both God-fearing persons, and although they were not taught to understand Scripture, they did rely on Jesus, and did their best to honor Him. I have no doubt we will all be together in eternity and have a wonderful relationship that we were unable to achieve on earth.

Meanwhile, by the time I was a teenager, I was a real rebel. I constantly got into trouble of one sort or another. My parents were religious, and regular church-goers. The family had to kneel in a circle each evening, and chant long meaningless prayers. Unfortunately, the denomination of Christianity my parents belonged to was strong on dogma and doctrine, but weak on teaching understanding and wisdom. The particular church we attended was all empty form and little helpful function. Looking back I see little evidence of the Holy Spirit, or the love of Christ. Surrounded by cant and hypocrisy, I rejected religion at age thirteen. I didn't know it then, but I had thrown out the Baby with the bathwater.

By then I was a liar and a thief. I stole a motorcycle and rode it all around the city. Eventually I was chased and finally stopped by a policeman. He said that if I hadn't been speeding he wouldn't have noticed me. So it was at an early age I became a bikie and got my first ticket.

Before my fifteenth birthday I had left school and started full-time work. Before my seventeenth birthday I had a motorbike, and before my eighteenth I had a fast, powerful bike and a V-8 car.

Early in my teens I had decided not to take life seriously until I grew up. I was into V-8's, motorbikes and girls. At the time I thought I couldn't get enough girls, but looking back I can see there were far too many, and I treated them badly. As for the cars and bikes, the road was a racetrack. Cops were just another hazard to be avoided. Speeding fines were just annoying taxes. Looking back I am amazed that I wasn't killed or jailed many times. I can see the hand of God protecting me from my own stupidity. Only God knows why He protected me, but I suspect that it was His response to my mother's faith in Him and her prayers for me.

At age twenty-one, I decided that it was time to take life seriously. I began to look for some way to make a fortune. That turned out to be a much harder task than I had imagined. I found that while I could get any number of jobs at the unskilled or semi-skilled level, it was not possible to find one that led to big money. I began to read more widely, and began a search for wisdom. That too turned out to be a much harder task than I had expected.

After three fruitless years I decided that I should go to a university. There, I thought, I was sure to find wisdom. Since I was looking for wisdom, it made sense to study philosophy. Since I had left school before my fifteenth birthday, I did not have a solid education and struggled with the academic requirements. The social life was exciting. Most students spent more time partying than studying and I was no exception. Four years later I took a Bachelor's Degree, majoring in philosophy. Though I had struggled with my studies, I had proved to myself that I wasn't stupid as I had been brought up to believe. I had also discovered that wisdom was not to be found in the Philosophy Department, and I suspected that it was not to be found anywhere in the university.

So it was that at age twenty-eight I had an education, a house, a car, a wife and a baby, but I still had neither wisdom nor wealth. There were some good jobs offered to me, but they were all long-term propositions. I wanted something with better prospects for the good life before I got too old to enjoy it. One of my brothers, who was a foreman in a factory, had managed to save some money and was also looking for something better. We joined forces and bought a service station and motor repair business. We did very well and soon built a level of affluence that neither of us had previously known. One day the bank manager came calling to ask if we would like to borrow a large sum for a project. We certainly were doing well! Little did I know how soon I was to lose it all.

One day a beautiful young woman came in to have her car serviced. I just had to have her, and pretty soon we were having an affair. This was not the first time I had cheated on my wife, but the others were just out for a good time, too; and my wife didn't seem to worry when I was out late. She spent a lot of time with her friends and seemed happy with that. There had never been any passion or romance in our marriage. We were really just companions. Starved for love as a child, I had for many years been looking for love in the arms of women. When my baby daughter came along I had decided to stop all that, but now I was reverting to my former ways. I never found satisfaction.

Looking back I can see what a rotten person I was. I was a liar, a cheat, and very selfish. Knowing from my own admission what a rotten person I was, you may find it very difficult to believe what I am about to tell you. Over the years, I read and heard about several such accounts as this, and I wrote them all off as flights of fancy or delusions. I scoffed at anything that hinted of a knowing, caring God out there. And yet strangely, I was always ready to give credence to tales of E.S.P. I suspected that most religions had some truth in them, but not much. I was pretty much New Age in my thinking and outlook. I was such a habitual liar that my mind could no longer distinguish between truth and falsity. If you can relate to what I am saying here, then you know how the mind can be swayed this way and that; it is only flesh after all. I can only advise that you to put your usual mindset to one side, and listen to your spirit, which knows the truth when it hears it.

One evening when I was with my lover, I had an over-powering desire to completely possess her. I was no longer satisfied with knowing her physically, I wanted my mind to enter her; I wanted my very awareness to be within her. I wanted to know her thoughts and feel her feelings. In order to do that, I forced my spirit to leave my body.

At this point some of you may be ready to write me off as a fruit-loop. Talk of out-of-body experiences can affect people that way. You need to understand that we all have two bodies: the physical one you are familiar with, and a spiritual 'body' that the soul cannot be separated from. This spiritual 'body' has no mind of its own anymore than a physical body does. Mind is part of soul, along with emotion and volition. I can only tell you that I was familiar with 'out-of-body' experiences, but that I had never before tried to enter another person. Well, I didn't succeed. I left my body, but instead of entering her I found myself surrounded by featureless grayness. I think at that moment, I died. My friend later told me that she thought I had died of a heart attack. One moment I was with her, fully engaged in what we were doing, and the next moment I was a lifeless hulk. To all intents and purposes I was lifeless for about forty minutes. My friend was skilled at first-aid procedures, and attempted to find a pulse or breath several times without success. Of course, I knew nothing of that until she told me later.

I felt puzzled rather than afraid. This was not like anything I had known before. In vain I looked in every direction, but could see nothing at all. I continued to scan, but it was impossible to focus as there was nothing to focus on.

Just as I began to feel panic, I noticed a faint glimmer off to one side. When I looked I could see nothing, but when I didn't look in that direction I had the sense of a very faint light off to my right. Sometimes when you look at the night sky you have the impression of stars, which are so dim you are not quite sure they are there. It was like that, only there was just the one glimmer.

Suddenly, I wanted very strongly for that glimmer to be a light. I found that I could move toward it, and I did so simply by willing it. I had the impression of moving rapidly and eventually the glimmer became an undeniable light. At the same moment that I knew there really was a light out there, I realized that I was surrounded not by grayness, but by impenetrable darkness. It is as if one cannot see darkness unless there is some light to measure it by.

As soon as I recognized the darkness as such, I became very afraid of what might be hidden in it. All I knew was to move toward the light, but even that was scary because the light also uncovered me. The light illuminated more and more of the space about me until the darkness had shrunk to a small area behind me. It felt as though the darkness was trying to pull me back, and I had to keep willing myself further into the light.

There came a moment when I was aware of a kind of portal or doorway ahead of me. I could see no door, just an opening. The light was coming from beyond that opening. At the same time that I saw the source of the light, I stopped moving forward. I wanted to go through into the light as I felt that only then would I be safe. Try as I might I could not go forward, but I knew I only had to relax in order to go backward. I could still feel the pull of the darkness.

Looking more carefully at the opening, I saw that it had parallel sides, but was rounded at the top having a narrow appearance. The figure of a man appeared in the doorway. I thought the doorway and its occupant were about 50 meters away from me until He stepped forth. Suddenly my perceptions changed as I realized that He was gigantic in comparison with me, and quite a long way from me. It seemed to me that I was no taller than the soles of His sandals. I was terrified. Amazingly, with each step He took toward me, He seemed to shrink.

34

When He came near me He was just a little taller than me. He stood there, about ten meters away, and gazed at me. There was nothing disdainful in the way He looked at me, but His gaze contained complete knowledge of me. He saw all of me. He knew everything there was to know about me.

Now I was even more terrified because His revealing gaze showed me what a filthy rotten bit of muck I was. Every willful and wrong thing I had ever done was revealed for what it was. Every selfish and uncaring word or action, every lie, distortion of truth, or rejection of God and His Word was there to see along with its affects in people's lives.

As I saw myself revealed, I also saw that He was faultless and perfect in every way. Then He spoke saying, "You know Who I Am."

"But you are not real," I replied. And He just looked at me with that knowing look.

A feeling of great hopelessness came over me as I began to realize that this could be Judgment Day for me. What hope could there be for me? I had been living a life of sin. I had denied Christ for more that half my life, and had apparently died when in the very act of adultery.

"What do you want?" He asked. I knew very well that He knew exactly what I wanted, but He obviously wanted me to say so. "I want to go in there where the light is coming from," I said, without any real hope that I would be allowed to enter.

"You can't go in there, and you know why," He said with finality. At that, all remaining hope and strength drained out of me; I was in utter dread.

It was then, at the lowest moment of my entire existence, when there was not an ounce of pride or defiance left in me, the amazing grace of the Lord took me to the greatest moment of my life. He led me to a low bench that I had not noticed before, and sat down with me upon it. Drawing me close to His side He said, "Neavei, I love you."

I knew it was true because He said it, but also because I could feel it. I cannot describe that love except to say that it far transcends anything you can imagine. The most loving feelings you have ever experienced toward your own children pale in comparison. His love swept through me touching every part of me. I could not comprehend what was happening. For most of my life I had been denied love and now the Creator Himself was infusing me with His untrammeled love. Here was I, this vile mucky creature, being loved by this perfect Lord of All Creation — Jesus. I felt that I was being washed, touched, and healed. For a time I just bathed in glory.

By and by, my wits returned, but just as I began to wonder about the apparent contradiction of being turned away from the door and yet being loved by Jesus, He spoke again. "I am sending you back, for I have work for you to do," He said.

I could not reply; being completely overwhelmed with joy at this reprieve.

"There are many on earth who know of Me," He continued, "but they don't know My Word is true. Many have been raised in confusing circumstances and are deceived. They need to be told the Truth. You are to tell them, 'I Am. I love them. I Am coming back soon.'"

The Lord explained to me that being familiar with the Biblical stories about Him is not enough. The people have to know that the accounts of His life on earth, which are found in the gospels of Matthew, Mark, Luke and John, are true. He further explained that although He has many servants, there is much to be done. He said there were many people who needed to hear the truth from me. He said He would empower my words to touch people who could not otherwise receive the truth.

When He told me how many people I must reach for Him I was frightened. "Lord, I can't reach that many people. I'm only Neavei."

Assuring me that I could indeed accomplish the task He was giving me, He again stressed that many souls depended on the work I was to do. He explained that He could accomplish His will without my help, but preferred to do things this way.

"I must start this work right away," I said.

"You will not begin this work for many years," said the Lord. Then He went on to tell me of many things I would do over the next twenty years.

I was aghast at what He told me. "I won't do those horrible things, now that I see them for what they are," I protested.

Realizing the futility of arguing with an all-knowing God, I was filled with shame at hearing of these things I would do. He then explained that I would do these things because I would not remember the truth. I would not be able to remember. "There is no light in you, only darkness," said Jesus.

Puzzled and fearful, I asked how I would ever be saved, and how I would become an instrument in the salvation of others? The Lord Jesus then explained to me that the day would come when I would call out to Him to save me from the mess I had made of my life. He said that from that moment He would hold me in His hand, and the light would begin to dawn in me. As the light in me grew, memory of these experiences would come to me. Even then it seemed, I would tarry until the end of days when time was very short. How will I ever manage to reach so many people if I have so little time to do it," I asked.

"Trust in Me, for My timing is perfect. When the time comes, I will give you the means," He replied.

Even as I heard those words it seemed, I awoke to find myself face down in the back of the car. I remember gasping for breath, and then choking on the dust I had just breathed in. Pulling myself together, I stumbled out of the car only to be accosted by my friend. She had thought me dead, and had been pacing up and down wondering how to get rid of my body without facing awkward questions. She was married, too, and was fearful of the consequences should her husband discover what she had been doing. Now she thought it had been a bad joke on my part. I had just been pretending to be dead.

It took me some time to calm her and assure her, that I had no knowledge of what had happened. Indeed, that was true. Even as I tried to explain, I could remember only that I had been out of my body, and had some really great experiences up in the clouds. Thinking that it was only natural for me to be a little confused after being in some kind of coma for more than a half-hour, I said I would tell her everything in a day or two.

Even the vague memories I had awoken with were quite gone the next day. I knew I had experienced something quite mystical, but beyond that I had no idea what it had been. Many times, I tried to recall what had happened that night; I could not. I could remember the occasion and what I had tried to do, but beyond that — nothing. Only the conviction that something wonderful and frightening had happened, remained with me. So the years passed.

Through the passing of twenty years I did many things I am now very ashamed of. I have repented of those things, and ask forgiveness from all those I hurt. I was degenerate.

In the year of 1992, when my life was at an all time low, I called out to God. It was a desperate cry for help, but it came out in the form of a challenge. "Hey there Big "G", I don't know if You are real, but they say You are. I don't know if You can hear me, but they say You can. I don't know if You care, but they say You do. I want to know the truth! If You are real, and You are who they say You are; I don't understand why The Creator of the whole Cosmos would care about a nothing hopeless failure like me. I want to know the truth! If You are real; if You sent Your Son Jesus to live as a man, and die on the cross to save us from our sins, then reveal Yourself so I may know the truth."

I did not notice any sudden change. I had not expected to. I thought the whole proposition was absurd — just another sign of the deluded state I was in. I put the matter out of my mind.

Weeks passed, and I found myself sharing a house with a Christian. He had answered my advertisement for a flat mate. We had some common interests, and enjoyed the same shows on television, so we got along quite well. He seemed an ordinary bloke in most ways, but one night a week, and twice on Sunday, he did something weird: He went to church. He always invited me but I never went. No way! I was not going to get mixed up in that kind of crap.

About the same time, my children started to talk about the things they were learning at the religious education classes at their school. One night my flat mate said, "I know you don't believe as I do. I would like you to come along to church just for fellowship and to enjoy the good music."

I accepted his invitation, but was completely unprepared for what happened. To my amazement there was a church full of people who were obviously enjoying themselves. That was a big enough shock, but soon I was listening to the preacher's message and something in me was responding. Afterward, my friend asked me if I had enjoyed it. I said I had in some ways, but I didn't want to go back again because it was too uncomfortable.

Months passed, and I would occasionally go to an evening service with my friend, but always with the same result. During this time, I was increasingly engaged with an internal debate. I did not know if I was talking to myself or if this was God I was talking to. There were changes in my life; I began to care about things I had not cared about for a long time. About that time I visited my sister, who had been a born-again Christian for some years. She witnessed to me, and also shared with me some information that my dad had given her. These things had a powerful effect on me. I wanted to believe in Jesus. He seemed to be the answer to so many problems. But, was all this just the delusions of an emotional cripple who couldn't make it without some sort of crutch?

One by one, the Lord dealt with the issues I raised. There came a time when I knew that I had to make a decision about the direction my whole future would take. For the greater part of my life up to that time, I had believed that there was no personal God. If there was a Creator, then He had done His work long ago, and left the whole universe to fulfill its destiny in some autonomous way. Now I seemed to be discovering that there is a God who knows, cares, and answers. In my search for wisdom I had looked into the most popular religions and some cults, and found them wanting. They were all dead, lifeless philosophies, which created more troubles than they solved. Now I was being confronted with a sovereign God who takes a personal interest in all who seek Him.

Now I prayed another prayer, "God, if You really are listening, and if You really do care, I want to know the truth no matter what it costs me."

It was as if blinders had been suddenly removed from my eyes. All around I saw evidence of God. In plants, animals, mountains, and especially in people, I saw things I had always been blind to. Previously, I had seen only the natural. Now I saw something of spirit in all creation. It was almost as if I could see the blueprint for each thing as well as the thing itself.

By this time I felt a great urgency to get the matter settled. One sleepless night I sat up with the Bible. I could not accept with my mind what I now know in my heart to be true. Early in the morning, I prayed, "God, I have reservations about what is written in this Bible. There are either contradictions in these books or I lack the ability to understand what I am reading. Show me, in a way I can understand, the truth about just one of these apparent contradictions and I will take the rest on trust until such time as You may reveal more to me."

Instantly I received an understanding of that particular puzzle. There and then I gave my heart to Jesus. Over the years since then, many puzzles have been sorted out for me.

Some weeks later I responded to an altar call, making my new faith a matter of public knowledge. Soon I was baptized with water. Then I received baptism of the Holy Spirit. I was saved, redeemed and made a part of the

Body of Christ. All that happened quickly, but now began the slow process of the renewing of my mind to conform with my status as a child of God. Slowly, I made progress in the things of God. I joined the Full Gospel Business Men's Fellowship International and fellowshipped with men who knew and loved Jesus.

There came a time when sufficient light was in me for memory of that wonderful event of twenty years ago to come flooding back to my conscious mind. It happens from time to time with anyone who has lived awhile, that a particular sight, or smell, or happening will remind one of a time or place that has not been thought of for many years. When that happens, one is not confused. The memory of that event is clear and one knows it as memory. Such is the case with the memory I have of those events of long ago. I have recounted them here as accurately as I am able. This is a true account of real events.

The good Lord continues to improve me as the Holy Spirit deals with me, changes me, and conforms me to Jesus. Praise God for the work He has done, and continues to do in our lives. The fact that you are reading this account proves that Jesus has given me the means to carry out the commission He gave me so long ago. I pray that Jesus blesses all who read this testimony and calls them to a closer walk with Him.

JESUS LIVES! The Bible stories about Him are true. Jesus loves us, and will save all who call on His mercy and receive Him into their hearts. These are "The Last Of Days." Jesus is coming back soon!

Kind permission was given to share this testimony from Living Connections Ministries (www.livingconnections.com).

CHAPTER 12

I Knocked At Hell's Gate
The Debra McFarland Story

I grew up in a house – not a home. Maybe you grew up in a "house" too, something like mine. A house is where four walls surround you. Inside those four walls is constant conflict and hurt. There is no love ... no hugging ... very few kind words. A home has kind, gentle, warm words of love ... a hug now and then ... laughter ... security ... warmth in relationships. I wish I would have had a *home* like that to grow up in, but it wasn't to be. Nevertheless, I am thankful that I at least had a house to grow up in. Some hardly even have that.

Through high school I was "blessed" with a counselor who essentially convinced me that I would never amount to much. I was continually being reminded that I was slow to learn. Have others somehow made you feel like you are slow and dumb? That is such a lie, because God accepts you for who you are. Don't let anyone try to convince you differently. Trust God to place you around children who need to hear you tell them that they are very special to God, and God has some special things for them to accomplish during their lifetime. You may not realize what your words of encouragement will do in the mind of a little child.

When I was in the eleventh grade in school, my fragile world became even more shattered. My father had been in the hospital for some time. He had cirrhosis of the liver due to alcohol abuse, though I didn't know it until later on in life. Every day after high school, I would go to the hospital and visit him. I loved him so much. I asked Jesus over and over not to let my father go away. He looked so terrible. But I believed Jesus would make him better. At certain times he would say to me, "Debbie, I love you. I'm truly sorry. I'm really sorry. Please forgive me." I really didn't know what to forgive him for.

My grandmother (whom I also loved very much) painted china, and she helped me paint a plate with a horse on it for my father. I took it to him and he was greatly pleased with the gift, but he didn't want it kept there at the hospital. He told me to take it home, and he would be coming home soon as well. I believed him.

The next day at school they called me to the office. The counselor that I admired so "greatly" broke the news to me about as cold as she could possibly have delivered it: "Your father is dead."

I refused to believe her. I was convinced she was lying to torment me. *"I just saw him yesterday! He said he is coming home! He's not dead!"* I was almost delirious and near shock.

"No – he's dead," came her cold retort. "Accept it."

I fell over on the floor. The pain was just too much for me to bear. All I could do was ask, "Why Jesus, why? I loved my dad so much. Why? Everything I love goes away." Have you ever felt that way?

After that ... I began to think to myself that maybe I shouldn't love.

Years passed, and I managed to graduate from high school and then started attending college. I had a vacuum inside me though. I wanted someone to love, and someone who would love me. I was vulnerable. It was classic: I was attracted to men who abused me. All I had known was abuse growing up, and I didn't feel I deserved any better as I grew older. It's a classic lie from the devil. It's a total and complete lie ... I know *now*. I just didn't know it then.

I became pregnant and was counseled to have an abortion. I knew it was wrong, but the pressure to go through with it was more than I could stand up against. I was taken to an abortion clinic by my soon to be husband in Detroit, Michigan. There were a number of women there waiting to have abortions as well, and they acted as if it's an everyday thing, which I guess to them it was. I felt so alone and so afraid. I felt like I was in an assembly line. I did not want to kill my baby inside me; I was so confused in my head. I didn't know what I should do. When it was my turn, the nurse took me to a changing room and I changed into a gown. As I stood, there my heart was racing. I peeked down the hall, snuck out and tried to run away. One of the nurses caught me and took me back, saying, "I don't think you should do this." You see, the money was already paid. I think I remember asking Jesus to forgive me. I know I did later and always for a lot of years, until someone told me you only need to ask once; Jesus forgets and the sin is no more.

I married the guy who got me pregnant. I didn't have anyone else to turn to, even though I didn't love him. He went into the Air Force. I became a military wife. We went off to Texas and I lived there for six weeks. His neglect and abuse of me grew worse. He got an assignment in Greece, and we spent two years there. He was a military policeman. He grew more hardened, at least around me. There was more physical abuse along with the verbal abuse.

When his two-year tour was finished in Greece, he got reassigned to the United States again. I got pregnant with my first child. I had a little girl, named Rachael. She was so special. Then a boy came along. We named him Phillip. By the time Phillip came along, the pain in the marriage was nearly at the bursting point. My husband had an affair, but because I simply refused to believe divorce was an option, I stayed with him. Then he had another affair (that I knew about anyway), and this time he wanted a divorce from me. I refused, but he filed for one anyway and it went through. He left me and our two children for awhile, but then came back with what appeared to be some compassionate concern. He suggested he take the two children for a month so I could have a rest. I thought it was a good idea, but the moment I stepped off

41

that military base, he got papers filed that I had abandoned my children. They were taken away from me.

Like so many times before, I asked, *"Why, Jesus? Why? What have I done so bad to be treated this way?"* Then in the confusion and hurt, I began to grow bitter at Jesus. I knew it was wrong, but I just couldn't help it. Are you holding bitterness against God right now? It's a carefully orchestrated attack by the devil to separate you from God. I learned that the hard way.

I met some girls and entered the party scene, drinking, and one night stands. I didn't care about my life. My ex-husband said I was dirt and subconsciously maybe I thought I was. My friend and I partied almost every night, and all weekend I drank a lot because I didn't care. No matter how much I sinned against God, the next day when I sobered up I would ask Jesus to forgive me. I would tell Him I was sorry for acting the terrible way I had acted the night before, and that I loved Him, and to help me. I would tell Him that I feel like a piece of a puzzle that didn't belong anywhere. *"Where do I belong Jesus?"* I would ask this over and over...

I took a barmaid job and began to grow hard. I swore and didn't care. I hurt people and didn't care. I used men and found pleasure in it – I felt power in it.

I had been going with my friends to a palm reader. This palm reader kept telling me things that were going to happen in my life, and I would believe her. I didn't care about the warnings the Bible gives about doing such things. I was blinded to the fact that this is a gateway to the demonic realm.

I was really tired one night from work and went to bed early. Around 3 a.m. in the morning I woke up sharply out of a hot sweat. At the foot of my bed stood two figures. I rubbed my eyes, saying to myself, *"Who is it? Who is there?"*

One figure was all dressed in black with a hood over its head. The other figure was all dressed in white. They were standing quite far apart. The figure in black kept shaking its head back and forth as if to gesture that I was a lost cause. The figure in white was waving to me and smiling-like. I kept rubbing my eyes because I wasn't really certain this was actually happening, or I was having some kind of delusion. Then in an instant they both disappeared. I dismissed the whole thing a few days later, though it left me with a very eerie feeling.

I kept living the same rebellious lifestyle after that. I didn't heed the warning. For some reason I went about half-an-hour early to the home of the girl that I partied with a lot. That was very unlike me. We left and went to Dunkin Donuts. My friend had a bottle of rum in the car and we both were drinking rum and Coke, our usual thing. I didn't want a lot of rum in my cup, because I was driving that night. That wasn't like me either because normally it didn't concern me how much I drank while I drove, nor she either, for that matter.

I remember putting on my seatbelt and we pulled out of the parking lot of

Dunkin Donuts and drove on down the highway. At the first stoplight, it turned red and I stopped. We were listening to music, and when the light turned green, I started forward. Then out of nowhere, a car was coming at us at high speed, running the light. I remember my friend yelling, "Oh, my God!" - just before the car hit us.

I left my body. I started going down this long, dark tunnel. It was dark ... so dark. I knew I was dead and I was going to hell. You couldn't even see the hand in front of your face. I was yelling, *"I don't want to go yet! I don't want to go yet!"* I'm falling farther and farther away from the little light at the top of the tunnel above me.

Out of the dark, things began grabbing at me. Long fingernails began to grab me and claw at me, trying to pull me into them. I kept screaming, *"No! I don't want to go yet!"* Their grotesque mouths were open wide and their teeth were gnashing at me. There was no sound coming from them though.

Then I began pleading with Jesus. *"Jesus, no ... don't let me go to hell! I'll do right! Please give me another chance. I'll do right!"* I begged and pleaded with Him.

Suddenly my body stopped and there was like a flash of light. It was like I was suspended in mid-air. Then I felt the impression of hands on my bottom, and the hands pushed me so fast. I saw myself going back toward the light at the top of the tunnel.

The next thing I remember is that I woke up in the hospital, but not in textbook fashion. At first my eyes were closed, and when I opened them up, looking around to see where I was, I was confused. I couldn't figure out exactly where I was. In my confusion, I then heard a policeman say, "Oh – we lost this one. Do you have her name – anything on her?"

I then opened my eyes wider and said, "No you **didn't** lose me!" He jumped back, scared out of his wits. The nurses and doctors came running in and the place was mass pandemonium. There is blood coming from me everywhere. They're pulling glass out of my body – there was a big piece above my eye. All I could do was lay there and sob, thanking Jesus for saving me from that dark pit I was in — being taken to hell.

After my bad accident I slowly gave up the party scene and the crowd and friend I hung with. My friends asked me why I was acting different and why I didn't want to party anymore; I told them God gave me a second chance at life and I didn't dare risk throwing it away anymore. I eventually moved and got back into church; I needed to start living by the principles of the Bible.

Friend ... you do **not** want to go where I was headed. You may **not** get the second chance I got. You had better get right with the Lord, because the next intersection may be your eternity. If my only purpose to be given a second chance at living was to write this and keep you from going to hell, then bless God and thank Him.

Get right with God ... is all I have to say.

CHAPTER 13

Dream Warning
The Pete McMaster Story

I lived with my parents on a farm in Western Victoria, Australia and was raised a Roman Catholic. Dad was pretty hard at times and would often drag me out of bed on Sundays to get me to church.

I remember one day, however, when I had decided to 'give church the flick.' I took off across the paddocks with my dad in hot pursuit, waving a cricket bat and shouting for me to stop! But with a mind of my own and plenty of determination, I kept running, that is until I heard him yell: "I'm going back 'fer the gun if you don't stop!" Dad always meant business and I remembered the gun hanging just above the back door in the house. It didn't take me long to come to the conclusion that it might be healthier if I just went to church, no matter how much I disliked going.

I started smoking cigarettes at around eight or nine and had my first joint of marijuana at fifteen. I played around with motorbikes and guns, preferring the outdoor life. After attending a country high school until year eleven I finally left when I was seventeen. To me, school was an easier option to carting hay or working in the woolshed. Despite failing most subjects, I managed to pass eleventh grade math.

Most of my boyish pranks were restricted to occasionally doing donuts on the local golf course or riding a motorbike through town slightly less than in a sober state. I didn't think this was too serious at the time.

By the age of 30, I was an alcoholic and drug addict. I didn't consider this too unusual though, because all of my mates were the same. I seemed to possess a natural dislike for work and spent a lot of my time drinking beer and smoking dope. I was either drunk or stoned most of the time.

One night I was sleeping beside my girlfriend when I suddenly woke up, panting and in a sweat. Waking her up, I said, "I've just dreamt that I'd been shot in the stomach!" She didn't seem too concerned and rather casually replied, "O yeah, good on 'ya," and went back to sleep. Two nights later I had exactly the same dream! Again, I woke up panting and in a sweat. "I just dreamt I've been shot in the guts *again!*" I exclaimed. This time my girlfriend took me more seriously.

It was Christmas Eve and a Friday night. I had decided to go around to a mate's place for a few beers. On the way, I remembered the dreams I had and recall thinking... *I hope I don't get shot in the guts tonight.* As we drank and talked into the night, my mate was playing around with a loaded shotgun. You guessed it. Suddenly it discharged! Realizing I had been hit in the stomach, I ran outside shouting, "Phil, you (lot of swear words); you've shot me!"

44

Although at first it didn't seem too bad, I soon felt a stream of blood running down my leg. Fortunately, the local hospital was just down the road, so I started towards it. By the time I got out into the street, however, I started going down. I thought: *I'm going to die, but at least I'll soon find out where you go when you do!* For some reason, I didn't seem too worried.

Others came to help and after loading me into the back of their van, they drove me off to the hospital. I heard the doctors whispering and knew the situation wasn't real good. I had pellets in my mouth, in my stomach, legs, hand, face and right ear. After they removed the gunshot, I laid awake for three whole days. The morphine drip was not in properly and I was in agony. I had staples in my stomach from the top of my groin to my chest where they had done an operation. I really thought I was going to die of pain then. Thoughts ran constantly through my head: *How come I had dreamt I was going to get shot? Was it some kind of premonition?*

I didn't give God a thought, because to me Christians were little more than a bunch of two-faced hypocrites who just loved to get dressed up on Sundays! Finally, a nurse gave me an injection and I slept for the next two days.

When I had recovered sufficiently to be discharged from the hospital, I focused on finding answers for *why* I had dreamed about being shot. I read about the predictions of Nostradamus; studied the teachings of psychics and channelers; anything I could get my hands on. However, despite all that had happened, I didn't stop drinking beer or smoking dope.

Before long I started believing what I was reading. I took a particular interest in anything to do with the end of the world. I read about Armageddon and studied Eastern religions, but still had no interest personally in Jesus Christ, nor most of the Bible.

One day I saw an advertisement in a magazine. The caption read: "Do you want to know the secrets of the Universe?" I thought: *That sounds alright,* so I wrote them and they sent back books and information on certain rituals I could perform. I would set up a mirror with candles and an altar and recite a prayer. It wasn't a prayer to the true Creator of the Universe, but "to the god of the Cosmos." At the time, it all sounded harmless enough. Later however, I discovered that the Greek word for *Cosmos* was World. So in effect, I was praying to the god of this World who is Satan. 2 Corinthians 4:4 says, "...the god of this world hath blinded the minds of them which believe not, lest the light of the glorious gospel of Christ, who is the image of God, should shine unto them."

After praying the prayer I started shaking and remember thinking: *This is strange! What's going on here?* I soon became filled with pride. Everyone else was wrong and I was right. I continued drinking beer and whiskey which led me down an even darker path as I drew closer into demonic, occult practices.

By now I was growing more desperate in my search to find truth. I had become paranoid about the end of the world. I buried food in case there was a catastrophe. I was tiring from all the false predictions I was being fed. There were date settings and predictions, but from which nothing ever eventuated.

These "so called spiritually enlightened teachers" also taught you how to leave your body (called astral projection). I tried it a couple of times but that was enough. It was a strange experience to be actually out of your body while it was still lying on a bed!

I also looked at Buddhism and Hinduism, but to me their teachings were complicated and unreliable. Neither made any sense as far as I was concerned.

It was at this point I finally started thinking about God, and to try and learn more about Jesus. After all, I had looked at all the other religions with their alternative thinking and none had offered me any helpful answers.

I became especially interested in biblical prophecy, finding particular interest in a book that had been written by a man called Barry Smith. I found his writings more reliable and informative than others. I was still not into reading the Bible however, except the book of Revelation and the book of Daniel.

When I finally decided to stop reading all the other New Age material, something inside me started to stir. I became depressed, anxious and fearful. I heard noises in my head. I couldn't think, read a book, watch television or do anything. I became a total wreck! I even wondered if I was going mad and whether others suffer like this. I just didn't know what was happening. Even so, I continued my drinking and smoking of marijuana.

One day I picked up another Christian book with what is commonly known as "the sinner's prayer" in it. Through this prayer, you invite Jesus into your life. I did this, but felt no different. It said that Jesus would set you free and I sure wanted to be free! So I kept on asking Jesus to set me free. I would recite the Lord's Prayer over and over. By now I was close to having a nervous breakdown. There was a struggle going on inside me; a spiritual battle was raging between the forces of good and the forces of evil, and I needed to be released from whatever it was that was trying to control me. *(Satan's desire for my soul, in all actuality)*.

One night at around 2 a.m., I went outside to see why the dog was barking. We lived in the Australian bush and it was not uncommon for the dog to bark at wallabies or other animals in the night. Going back to bed, I tried to get to sleep, but the dog's continual barking kept me awake. As I lay there in my wakeful state, I decided to amuse myself with a mind game I often played. The idea was to empty your mind, and then ask a question. The answer would be the first thought that came back into your head. So I asked what was the exact time and the answer came as *4:17*. I thought . . . that's strange; why would I think that when it's only 3:30 a.m.?

So I tried again and this time the word *Matthew* came to mind. I realized that Matthew 4:17 was in the Bible. As it was a Sunday morning, I got out of bed and looked it up. It said, "...Repent: for the kingdom of heaven is at hand." I found this rather interesting and mentioned it to my girlfriend. "Perhaps God is telling me something and maybe we should go to church?" was my response.

Although this was something we would never have imagined doing, we went off to church. After we got there we both became quite "emotional." Half off our trolleys from smoking dope, we saw what we thought was nothing more than a bunch of weirdoes waving their hands about in the air! Yet they seemed happy enough. We stayed as long as we could, but eventually left. Although glad to get out, I still intended on coming back the following week. This was a pattern we actually repeated for the next three months!

The Sunday morning that the pastor invited me to the front and asked if I wanted to become a Christian, I thought, *What are you talking about, mate? I've been coming for three months. I'm dressing up and everything. I thought I already was one!* Yet something inside me relinquished and I flippantly thought, *Yeah - whatever.*

I started repeating the sinner's prayer after him when I suddenly began shaking. I felt something in me trying to resist. Finally I made a confession and invited Jesus to be Lord of my life. The resistance I had been experiencing suddenly stopped and I felt free for the first time in my life! I was what the Bible calls becoming *born again.* "Jesus answered and said unto him, Verily, verily, I say unto thee, Except a man be born again, he cannot see the kingdom of God.... Except a man be born of water and *of* the Spirit, he cannot enter into the kingdom of God. That which is born of the flesh is flesh; and that which is born of the Spirit is spirit. Marvel not that I said unto thee, Ye must be born again." (John 3:3, 3:5-7).

Then, the noises started coming back. It was like someone had left a wireless on in the next room and I knew the enemy was trying to tempt me back to my old habits.

A visiting evangelist came to our church and invited anyone who wanted a special touch from God to come out to the front. I went out and he asked me what my problem was. I answered, "My mind keeps wandering." Immediately he rebuked the demonic spirit that was tormenting me. *"You lying, tormenting spirit, be gone in the Name of Jesus!"* he commanded, and it did! I dropped to the floor and everything went real quiet. From that moment, I knew I could fully trust God to remove all my anxieties and fears as well as the guilt and the shame of my former life.

My only desire now was to share the gospel (Jesus Christ died for our sins) with others. After what God did for me, I just wanted others in my position to also be free. I knew they could if they, too, were prepared to trust God by inviting Jesus into their lives, then begin trusting Him to set them free from the demonic strongholds that keep them bound and from walking in fuller dimensions of joy, peace and faith in God. I love God and I'm not afraid to share my faith with anyone anywhere. God has given me a strong gift of boldness. Jesus died on a cross for my sins and I want others to know about His love. God wants me telling others about His love.

I know I am saved and going to heaven, not because of anything great I have done but because of what Jesus has done *for* me. The only part I played was to simply believe what the Bible says about Jesus and allow Him to be first place in my life... every day, and that can be very difficult at times for every Christian believer, if they'll be honest.

Many people hear the truth that Jesus Christ died for their sins, so they trust in Him to save them of their sins. That's just the *beginning* of a normal, healthy relationship with the living God — the Creator of the universe. Yet the devil will do everything in his power to try keeping those infant believers in that spiritual state. He'll do everything he can to try to keep them in their "baby crib" all the years of their life, and never grow up and become productive Kingdom adults ... useful for the Master to work through to help rescue lost souls bound for hell. Just like my soul, I was headed for hell. For the most part I was so much under Satan's control, I didn't even *care* that my soul *was* bound for hell!

I pray that you will not just make Jesus *your* personal Savior, but invite Him to be *Lord* of every area of your life. To pick and choose areas you'll allow Him to be Lord of is a very dangerous place to remain in for very long. Either He can be trusted to be Lord of *all* in our life, or Lord of *nothing*. What's it going to be for *you,* mate? Giving Him your *all* ... or just a token crumb or two now and then to appease a guilty conscience?   Please be wise, and give Him your *all*. You'll never regret it once you pass over into eternity, I can promise!

A few closing comments:

My wife, Poss, and I have been Christians now for six and a half years as of 2005.   For fifteen years I lived out of a bag of clothes. Within three months of being saved, Poss and I got married because we knew that's what God wanted. We almost own our home now and there are no longer drugs or alcohol being used. God is doing great things in our lives and we just want to learn more of how we can serve and love Him. The former things have passed away. God has made all things new. We keep pressing on with the help of God through the demonic attacks all Christians come up against, and the old sinful flesh that never seems to want to die to its own selfish demands. Poss and I haven't "arrived" by any means, but from where we started out, God has brought us a long, long way! Thank you so much, Lord!

CHAPTER 14

Jump For Jesus
The Gene Sullivan Story

Gene Sullivan was born August 29, 1947 in San Francisco, California, as one of two sons to Prescott and Patricia Sullivan. Prescott was San Francisco's leading sports columnist for over fifty years with *The Examiner*. Patricia was a captain in the Army Aircorp during WWII and flew B-25 Bombers as a ferry pilot. After Gene was born, the two were divorced, and Pat went to Colorado and got involved in the airport management and crop-dusting business. Gene and his brother Mark were taken to their grandparents, where they stayed for three years. It was during this time that Gene's belief and relationship with God began. The boy's grandmother saw to it that they attended Catholic mass and instruction regularly. Gene says that from the time he began going to mass until committing his life totally to Jesus, he was very much aware that God had a plan for him and that God was very much aware of him and the things he did.

In 1956, the two boys were moved to Rifle, Colorado, with their mother. Growing up on the airport and being involved with the spray company was a very exciting and intense atmosphere. Even though Gene's relationship with God continued and God would answer prayer, Gene's life was not much of a testimony. Life was lived hard, dangerously, and with little concern about what God thought, or anybody else for that matter.

After graduation from high school, Gene entered the Navy for four years. As a flight deck director and fire fighter aboard the aircraft carrier Hancock, he made two trips to Viet Nam. During this time he also became the 7th Fleet heavyweight boxing champion and went on to win several titles, which ranked him among the top ten heavyweights in the nation. After Gene's discharge in 1969 he coached the Navy boxing team in San Francisco until a man called Evel Knievel came to town. Gene's dad was doing a story on Knievel and made the mistake of asking if he would like to meet the famous daredevil. Three days later Gene had quit his job and gone on the road with him.

Over the next two years, Gene was to be Evel's right-hand man, body-guard, and setup man. Knievel's commitment to his death defying cause was attractive, because there was nothing phony about the man's dedication to overcome life's biggest threat... death! "The stunt business appealed to me because of the thrilling entertainment it provided the crowds and because it is devoid of phonies. Stunt performance leaves no place for pretense."

Because of Gene's desire to be an entertainer and be in movies, he saw value in having a real image, the type people could look at and see was not phony. It brought forth a tremendous amount of loyalty in Gene toward Knievel, the type of loyalty that saw Gene defend his friend from the Hells

Angels in the Cow Palace at San Francisco; that saw him wait hand and foot on his friend after crashes that put him on his back; that saw him silent even when his friend failed to be faithful financially to him. The time came for Gene to choose between going out on his own in the stunt business or staying with Knievel.

About a month later Gene decided to leave Knievel, and go out on his own. He was back in Reno for a few days when a man invited him to a breakfast sponsored by the Full Gospel Business Men's Fellowship. "Although I wasn't especially religious I'd go anywhere for food, so I accepted the offer. Gene actually said to Ben Kinchlow on the 700 club, "You know the Lord tells us in the Proverbs, to depart from evil, so I did. I obeyed His Word and departed from Evel." It was a good laugh.

I stuck out like a sore thumb at the breakfast. Not only was my lifestyle 180 degrees opposite most of the men, but my size set me apart from everyone else. At that time I weighed 240 pounds, was lifting more than 400 pounds, and served as a nightclub bouncer in my spare time. The physical contrast between the speaker and I was hilarious.

The program committee had called in Albie Pearson, the smallest baseball player in the major leagues, to give the message. Pearson stood about five feet four and was known as "The Littlest Angel" when he played for California. Albie talked about establishing a personal relationship with Jesus, then introduced a friend who shared his personal testimony. What a story the man told! He had been a hard core heroin addict for six years, but when the Lord entered his life he just threw away all his drug-related paraphernalia. He said, "I want to tell you that I woke up the next morning a free man. I haven't had a single withdrawal symptom. God totally delivered me."

Gene said, "Two things happened to me when I heard about God's power in the speaker's life. First, I began to weep; second, I saw that everything I had done in life added up to zero. All my efforts to live up to high character standards were worthless in the sight of God, nor was He impressed with my ability to ride bikes through walls of fire, or any of my talents and abilities. He had brought me to the end of myself; I saw the vanity of life, my life without Jesus."

"…Verily, verily, I say unto thee, Except a man be born again, he cannot see the kingdom of God." (John 3:3).

When Albie Pearson invited those who wanted to receive Jesus as their Savior and Lord to come forward, Gene stood to his feet. My prayer went something like this: *Lord, whatever I am now, whatever I will be, wherever I go, whatever I do, I now totally commit my life into Your hands. You will be my Lord from this day forward. I want You to lead me in everything I do each day.* In my mind I visualized myself signing the bottom line of a contract. I had signed my life away to the Navy before, and I knew what it was like to "be owned" by the government. I knew I was signing my life away to Jesus, and

He would be the guiding force and provider of all my needs from that day forth. I knew my life was no longer my own, BUT HIS, to do with as He willed. When the prayer ended, I belonged to God.

"But ye shall receive power, after that the Holy Ghost is come upon you..." (Acts 1:8).

"Now, brother," Albie said, "we are going to lay hands on you and God will fill you with His Holy Spirit." Gene didn't have the slightest idea what that meant but he was sure it would happen. Sure enough, four men laid their hands on him and he began to speak in an unknown tongue. "I felt as though scales had fallen from my eyes and I could see the difference between right and wrong more clearly than before. I knew I should give up the wild partying I'd enjoyed for so long, and it wasn't a problem for me. I wanted to give those things up."

"...If any *man* will come after me, let him deny himself, and take up his cross daily, and follow me, For whosoever will save his life shall lose it: but whosoever will lose his life for my sake, the same shall save it. For whosoever shall be ashamed of me and of my words, of him shall the Son of man be ashamed..." (Luke 9:23, 24, 26).

For a time he returned to the stunt business, all the while asking the Lord to make him a faithful witness for Him. Opportunities came from every direction, television and movie contracts, performances before huge crowds. He had a contract for a million and a half dollars that he had signed in the stunt business. Then the Lord pulled Gene out of the public eye to prepare him for something better. One morning He was reading the Bible and the Lord said, *"Gene, I want you to give up everything."* He saw that Jesus was really taking him up on his promise at the breakfast meeting in Reno. He knew it was Jesus speaking to him in his heart.

"My sheep hear my voice, and I know them, and they follow me:" (John 10:27).

He obeyed God's voice, that spoke to his heart even though it didn't make financial sense to walk away from so much money. He also knew God's ways are not man's ways; God's thoughts are not man's thoughts. He called his manager and canceled the contracts. In a single phone call He walked away from the one thing in life he knew how to do. God was now his only guarantee of security. "There is a man that makes himself poor, but has great riches." He was about to buy the gold Jesus talks about in Revelation 3, the gold of WALKING IN FAITH, that is tried by fire. He knew he was not to lean on his own understanding, but trust in the Lord with all of his heart.

"So likewise, whosoever he be of you that forsaketh not all that he hath, he cannot be my disciple." (Luke 14:33).

A few weeks later he went to work as a shipping clerk for a Christian magazine, and mowing lawns for a church lawn service. Nobody there seemed impressed with his press clippings; no one cared about his boxing records and

51

skills with a bike. They were not moved by his physical abilities, that had gotten him everything in the world. For two and a half years his chief claim to fame was setting up overhead projectors for Bible teachers, and being the low man on the totem pole of the lawn service.

He had to stay in the meeting to shut off lights, etc., so night after night he was exposed to the truths of Scripture. Faith comes by hearing the Word of God, and His faith muscles began to grow, by being exposed to the anointed Word of God. The Lord knew that the rough edges of his life could be sanded smooth only by repeated encounters with the Word, and relationships with mature Christians. One lesson he needed to learn was that only the person who is faithful in little things can be trusted with larger responsibilities.

He saw being faithful in the small trivial things in life, and faithful to the least, was BEING FAITHFUL TO THE GREATEST, JESUS! Jesus' standard of judgment was not how we treat the greatest, but how we treat the little ones and the least esteemed. That's how we do unto Him. He began to see you can tell what people really believe and how much they really love Jesus, by how they treat the little ones.

Early in 1978 Gene began to pray seriously about his future work. God renewed the vision he'd had earlier about using a motorcycle to witness for Him. But Gene was filled with questions...*Where was I going to get a bike? How could I put together a show when I was nearly broke?* That's when the Lord gave him some basic training in faith. First he received an invitation to put on a program, then the Lord sent him a motorcycle. Gene began to get the picture. God was putting the whole ministry together so he couldn't take credit. He saw God's faithfulness to provide everything that pertained to life and godliness, and to go into the field Jesus was calling him into. Just like the Army always provided food, bullets and care, Jesus was a better provider than the Army, and certainly as faithful. He believed God's Word, "… yet have I not seen the righteous forsaken, nor his seed begging bread." (Psalm 37:25).

The Lord called him to use his talent of motorcycle stunt jumping to reach out with the gospel of His Kingdom to the lost. He had subjected his life to the disciplines of God, as taught by the men of God in his life. To be a disciple, is to be a disciplined one. When his obedience was fulfilled, he knew God wanted to use him to help others be disciplined, be discipled, obey God's voice, and Word. If we don't make God's thoughts our thoughts, and His ways our ways, then we can't really help others with their thinking and ways.

To make disciples, we have to be disciplined ourselves, trained to know God's ways, and hear His voice. "I was to go into the Church with my talent and my message and trust Jesus with the results. He greatly blessed it." In eight years, Gene was able to minister in over twenty-one denominations and has done 130 city-wide crusades. Nineteen years later, Gene did five programs in the Kingdom of Tonga for the King's birthday. His son, Wade, has come along with his own testimony, and is the newest disciple in using the Jump as a platform to give the testimony of Jesus.

"A man's gift maketh room for him, and bringeth him before great men." (Proverbs 18:16).

After twenty-two years of ministry, the fire the Lord had kindled at the breakfast in Reno, still burns brightly, and the reality of Jesus Christ is still as fresh and alive as that day. Gene's *food* is to share that reality with others and to see others set free and be saved and be kept by the power of God. He looks to hear from Jesus, everyday, and help those around him wake up to hear God's voice, too!

"...The voice of one crying in the wilderness, Prepare ye the way of the Lord, make his paths straight." (Matthew 3:3).

The kingdom of God is within us. We are living stones, and God uses master builders, which He being the Chief builder, to fit the stones together to make a building filled with the praise of God. Jesus is coming back for a bride that has made herself ready. Being ready has everything to do with Ephesians 4:11, and in receiving the apostles, prophets, evangelists, pastors and teachers God has sent our way. To speak the TRUTH to one another IN LOVE, so we can GROW UP, be complete, and prepared to meet THE KING OF KINGS, AND LORD OF LORDS, JESUS CHRIST. We should all be ones who are getting our act together, because we love the fact that Jesus will be appearing to us one day, and we will see Him face to face.

CHAPTER 15

The Day Satan Lost Our Family
The Neilja Harewood Story

By the end of this testimony, you will probably be laughing at the sequence of events that led up to "The Day Satan Lost Our Family." It all started with my mother. Mom was the youngest of eight children from a prominent family on a small island in the Caribbean. As children, they all attended Sunday school, then service with my grandparents.

My grandmother died when Mom was 12 and her dad married a not-so-nice woman. Nonetheless, my mother was able to grow into the wonderful person she is and always has been, even before giving her life to Christ.

One important fact I should mention is that many people in the Caribbean believe in, while others actually practice, the art of Obeah (also known as witchcraft, black magic or voodoo). Though our family was not involved in it, I can remember overhearing conversations between the adults about some bizarre occurrence they had heard about — the type of stuff you might see on *The Twilight Zone*.

By the time my dad started working with the Naval Air Defense, I was already grown with children. They moved into a brand new house in Philadelphia and had not been there long, when strange things started happening. For example, they would smell unusual foods cooking in odd areas of the house; hear unexplainable noises that were not necessarily eerie; and my brother, who was about six at the time, began acting very, very differently. Even his Pekinese acted weird.

As a result of her research, Mom found out that their house had been built on an Indian burial ground. Since I didn't live there and my parents are not social butterflies, I was never able to determine if other homeowners encountered similar things.

My dad, though he acknowledged something was happening, opted to totally ignore the entire situation. Mom, on the other hand, had no intention of living with whatever was in the house and resorted to the only course of action she could think of.

Somehow Mom obtained the name and telephone number of a Haitian woman who lived in New York and was supposedly well known as a voodoo queen. The woman came to the house and did whatever they do and left. Things were fine for a little while, then it all started all over again.

When Mom finally reached the woman again, she was out of the country and couldn't come personally, but could tell Mom what she had to do. Fortunately for her (or unfortunately, depending on whom you ask), my aunt was visiting at the time. So my mother, with my aunt behind her, my brother behind my aunt, the dog behind my brother and my father bringing up the rear, set out to "clean" the house. I wasn't there to see what they encountered. However, I can assure you they have no reason to lie about their experience.

That afternoon, while in my apartment in Brooklyn, I received a call from my mother and aunt. They told me about being physically attacked by something that was not visible to either of them. Mom received numerous scratches on her shoulders, neck, and face. My aunt was shoved down the stairs causing a pretty nasty bruise on her tailbone. When I saw her in October, 1998, she was still complaining about feeling soreness around that area.

When I saw them that weekend, Mom's scratches were still quite visible and my aunt was walking and sitting quite gingerly. What really made it sad was that they incurred these battle scars for no reason whatsoever. Whatever Satan had loosed in the house was greater than Mom, my aunt, my brother, the dog and my father combined, with the instructions of the "voodoo queen."

Since we're not talking about anything as extreme as the Exorcist, my parents continued living in the house. Some of the things, I thought were a little funny. For example, at night when my brother went to bed, Mom would tuck him in, say his prayers with him (as she had done with me as a child) and she would close his bedroom door behind her as she said goodnight. Once Mom left the room, the Pekinese (who I ultimately nicknamed the 'demon dog') would climb into my brother's bed, get under the covers and crawl to the foot of the bed, where he slept. The 5-6 pound dog would act like a rottweiller if anyone attempted to enter the room while my brother slept. If it was ever necessary for my parents to spank my brother, they would first have to lock the dog up or he would go absolutely insane. All the time my brother just kept acting stranger and stranger.

I don't recall exactly who or when it was, but someone told Mom that Satan could not drive himself out of the house. Only the power of God could help her. Though nightly prayers had always been part of Mom's routine, she started giving it some thought, and eventually decided to go in search of God. After a while, she found a very small, but growing, spirit-filled church with an anointed man of God as their pastor. She told him about the occurrences. So he and his tiny army of saints came over to pray for God's blessings on the house and its occupants. By this time she had already accepted Christ as her Lord and Savior with faith that was growing stronger with each passing day.

Need I say that now that Christ was a welcomed guest, Satan moved... real quickly. The occurrences stopped, and regretfully, the "demon dog" died shortly thereafter. My dad died some 20+ years later after struggling for a long time with his walk. However, praise God, he did eventually accept Christ's salvation before he died. Two years later Mom retired and moved to the suburbs of Orlando, Florida. She calls it 'God's waiting room.'

At 65 years old, her only concern about this move was her hopes of finding a nice church close to home. After all, she was one of the founding members and had been very active in the same church for 20+ years. By now the congregation had grown to over 3,000 members. So that was a major concern for her.

The fact that the only person she knew in Florida was the realtor (via telephone) and she had been there only twice before her move, none of this was of any consequence, because she knew God was with her *entire* being. The first time she was in Florida was when she flew down to select the site and the house. The second time was when I met her there for the closing. Her third trip was a few days after she retired and we both headed south on Interstate 95 with the moving company's truck behind us. That was about 4 years ago.

My mother, an 'anti-social butterfly,' is now on the Board of Directors of the Homeowners Association of the sub-division. It's comprised of people of all ages and races from the newly married with young children to the retired couples. She is very active in the community. If her neighbors don't see her walking her dog every morning (I recently got her a Maltese for company), then they ring the bell to make sure she's all right. I rest comfortably knowing that there are people nearby who truly care. You can't imagine how peaceful it is to know this, particularly since I am on the opposite end of the country.

As for the church. God is GREAT! She has found another small, and once again, growing house of worship that's less than a mile from the house. Believe it or not, she even likes it more than the one she left behind. Our Lord God Almighty has rewarded my mother's absolute, unwavering, blind faith in Him, once again.

I know you're not laughing yet, but wait — the best is yet to come. Had Satan left Mom alone, she would have continued to live like so many other people who are genuinely good-natured, kind-hearted people, that if asked, would say that they are Christians. Yet, they will have no understanding how they wound up in hell.

Poor Satan was too stupid to know that my mother was not about to tolerate his nonsense, even during her life in the world when she wouldn't have known to attribute the problems to him. He never expected she would seek the Great One. And, because of what came to be a *strong* faith and belief in God, he ultimately lost the rest of her immediate family, some of her brothers and sisters, nieces and nephews as well some of the many people whose lives she touched over the years.

Now, this is where it gets funny. About 8-9 years ago, prior to Dad's death, God revealed her ministry to her. He spent time preparing her, and though she did His bidding, she prayed and begged Him to reconsider His decision (she says it's physically draining). She even thought that possibly, once she moved to Florida, He might give her the answer she had been asking for. Well, He didn't, so she stopped asking. You see, His plan was to use her to combat that which initially took her in search for His face. And, as always, His plan is perfect.

Satan really blew this one. He permitted his presence to disturb the wrong person this time and it ultimately cost him a lot of souls. The one he messed with has turned out to be an armed soldier, whose job it is to boot him out wherever and whenever our Lord tells her to. For years my mother has had a *powerful* deliverance ministry.

That is how Satan lost our family: my Mom and Dad, their children and their grandchildren. This is three generations doing His bidding.

For those of you who don't know Him, I have no words that are sufficient enough to express the joy and wonders of serving a loving, living God. It's one of those things you just have to experience yourself, and I pray that one day you do.

CHAPTER 16

He Sent a Man To Free Me
The Ceci Sullivan Story

Isaiah, a great prophet in the Bible said, "Who *is* among you that feareth the Lord, that obeyeth the voice of his servant, that walketh *in* darkness, and hath no light? ..." (Isaiah 50:10). Well, I met a prophet (one who sees), and receiving him, opened my eyes to see things I never had seen before! God sent me a gift, and wrapped it up in the package of a man, and it took a great deal of faith to receive him. This man was a world class stunt man, and a champion heavyweight boxer. He had a famous father whom Walter Matthau portrayed in the movie *The Odd Couple*. His mother was an Army Aircorp pilot, who ferried B-25's during WW II. She and her partner owned a crop-dusting business in Colorado, the state I grew up in. None of these things are what makes this man so special, however. He's special because he was the one God personally sent my way! Meeting him has changed the direction and destiny of many lives, significantly and forever! Please, let me explain.

I've watched him fight the good fight of faith. His life has been a book of faith for me to read day by day. I have watched his faithfulness to God and God's faithfulness to him. He has helped spiritual wimps become spiritual fighters. I've watched fat people lose weight and become fit. I've met anorexics who have put on weight. I've watched people who were killing themselves by getting drunk on many of life's ills, reach sobriety! I've seen careless, mean men learn how to love, care and cover their wives and families. I've watched quiet, withdrawn, indifferent older couples learn to have love, passion and fire in their once bitter-cold relationships. Many years of bitter critical thoughts and offenses that had gone undealt with, made them worlds apart. They got answers for their unresolved offenses; they talk about their problems and fears, and have fallen into true love and faith. I've known a man who was insane and unable to relate to others, who learned to bring order to his life and thoughts, and to give and receive love.

I met a seventy-eight year old man, bedridden for fifteen years, unable to care for himself or relate with anyone, who was resurrected from his dead condition. I saw him learn to give and receive the love of God. He not only began using the bathroom, but became self-sufficient, and thrilled that God in His goodness led him to repentance. He faced his selfishness and changed the way he thought, and decided to love God and others before his life was spent in his hell of self-pity. He went from living by his senses and selfish desires to living life to glorify God. He ended up with the testimony of Jesus, rather than glorifying the works of the evil one.

I met a minister, full of pride, lying, selfishness and anger, who repented for oppressing God's people for years. He never wanted to see the correlation between loving those who are begotten of God, and loving God. He repented from being angry, hateful and indifferent, to being kind, caring and truthful with the men Jesus brought into his life. I met a rich woman who was eating and shopping herself to death (to avoid life's problems); her God was her belly, not Jesus. She repented and changed her mind. She has lost over 100 pounds, along with her world of lying, confusion, loneliness and selfishness! She received the people Jesus sent into her life to help her war against the enemies of her soul.

I've met whores who lived to seduce and have power over men, who had repented and learned to be givers and helpers, rather than takers and users. I've met slobs living in filth and self-indulgence, who have learned to live in restraint and to care for others. I've seen depressed, suicidal women, who were smoking themselves to death. They were killing themselves, starving themselves, sticking their finger down their throat, because they cared mostly about how they were being loved and accepted, not how they were loving and accepting others. They have become givers instead of being takers and users.

The thing all these people had in common is, they saw and received the ones Jesus sent into their lives to help them, and they learned to love and receive one another in honesty and sincerity. Jesus promised to send prophets among us. He also said we would lightly esteem, reject, kill them, and build their graves. I had to be deeply honest with myself, and as my spirit burned within me, I knew God had caused this man who had understanding to the deep things of God to cross the path of my life. His name is Gene (of noble birth) Sullivan (single eye). My name Cecile, means blind in one eye, and Jesus said, if your eye is single, your whole body will be filled with light. For the first time in my life, in 1986, my eye was single and I met a man whose whole body is filled with light, because he cares about pleasing God in what he thinks, says and does. He cares about the effect and influence he has towards others, and teaches others by his example. To God be all honor, praise and glory!

I'm the daughter of an Episcopal priest. My father, who is not alive now, was dead while he lived in his role as a father. He was addressed as Father Strange, and his name was Harvey Strange. As far as I could tell, he was a stranger to Jesus. Though he went through years of seminary, and theology and psychology, and gained the title of Priest, he never learned how to be one to his own children or God's children. He spoke several languages, but he probably seldom told the truth in any of them. He was overcome by every vice in life — drinking, smoking, overeating, inordinate sexual indulgence, and he was extremely overweight. He was never an example of a faithful over-comer, and died alone in his trash, filth, and hundreds of books. He was ever learning, but never came to the knowledge of the truth. He and my mother divorced when I was two years old, and he was a stranger to me.

I was number six out of seven children, and my mother remarried a man named Jim when I was nine years old. He had no idea how to cope with children, and though he attended church faithfully, he didn't have a clue how to reach me. He was a cold, indifferent, critical man, and he had no father, spiritually or carnally, to show him how to love children. Though he fulfilled outward obligations and duties, he constantly was inwardly cursing me. He had a relationship with his religious ceremony, and not Jesus — the Way, the Truth, and the Life! As he was dying of cancer when I was 16, his heart was broken because he knew he hadn't known Jesus and wasn't able to impart the spirit of life to us. I forgave him, then he died.

Our home always had people in it, but I was a desperate, lonely, deceitful and pitiful little girl. No one really knew where I was at, or how to help me. We attended church regularly, read to God, and told God and each other what we thought we should to keep the family boat from rocking. We were religious and deceitful. I watched the adults hold bitterness and offenses in their hearts, and I imitated them well, as children do. Jim had no idea how to deal with his anger, and he lit one Camel filterless cigarette after another. He was constantly aggravated, and I was always feeling rejected. We cared mainly for how we were all being affected selfishly by each other, and we didn't have answers to help one another. We didn't care that we didn't care!! The emphasis was trying not to be part of the problem because there was emotional abuse and abandonment to pay if you were part of the problem. It was life without Jesus, life without passion and love, but we went to church every Sunday.

I seemed to expose much of the emotional and spiritual things that we were hiding. So many parents excuse themselves and accuse their children. Not much was learned in our suffering, and I knew I would be doomed to repeat my parents mistakes if I didn't look to Jesus for help. I didn't talk about what was going on inside of me. Being open and honest with love and faith, wasn't part of the game plan. There was an atmosphere of fear especially regarding Jesus having the provision to meet our material needs. I always felt it was a hardship for my parents to provide for me and I transferred this into my relationship and beliefs about Jesus. My brother taught me to steal; fear and torment were normal to me. I've found that those who don't have faith for Jesus to satisfy their needs, will always steal in one form or another, even if it's affection that's not right.

When I was eight years old, I went to see the movie *Bambi* with my older sisters. I went into the bathroom during the movie, and a man held me at gunpoint and took me upstairs to sexually molest me. He told me he would kill me if I screamed. I had no idea what sex was. He pulled down his pants and I ran down the stairs, expecting to get shot in the back. I was taken to the hospital, then I spent the next two days in the police department looking at mug shots of molesters. I think that is when fear and torment became "normal" to me. It's as if thinking it's normal to be in a concentration camp. It's like having a bad guy living with you in your house that everyone is indifferent towards, and familiar with.

When I was 13, I thought all the family problems were because of me, so I ran away from home. I was convinced I wasn't worthy of my stepfather's love. I was looking for love in all the wrong places. I dated older men. I was looking for the comfort of a father that little girls long for, and when they don't receive it, they often look somewhere else for it. I didn't know the comfort of my Father in heaven or on the earth. In Ezekiel 16:4 it says that s*he wasn't swaddled, clothed, or washed* (emotionally and spiritually). I was a lost, rebellious, little girl with no one to give me the correction of the Spirit. They weren't led by the Spirit of Jesus.

We had a form of religious peace, but it was not God's peace, the peace that comes from having honest, open, sincere and humble relationships with one another. We told each other what we wanted to hear to keep the artificial peace. We went to church and read to God, because we thought it to be the "right" thing to do. We fulfilled outward obligations and duties, birthday cards, presents, and the observation of special days. We didn't know how to deal with bitter, critical, offended thoughts with each other, so the "special days, were never very special." We went to church, but we had life without God's help to deal with the divisions, accusations and evil imaginations in our hearts. No one knew how to fight the good fight of faith and love, so we avoided each other, avoided the problems, and had a pleasant way of lying to each other to keep the artificial peace. At age 14, I left this lonely family that I could never graft into because of pretense. I was a desolate heart looking to use men to get what I needed and letting them use me.

At age 18, I met Dr. Jekyl and Mr. Hyde, and fell in lust with him. He was cute and what I thought to be a "good Catholic boy." *(I didn't know about the murderer and rapist who was lying dormant within his soul, waiting for the opportunity to appear.)* Years later, Michael was referred to as the "Ted Bundy" of Colorado. (Ted Bundy was a notorious serial rapist and murderer.) This is when my nightmare really began.

I was working for my friend's mother. She and her husband owned a large apartment complex. I had a variety of jobs that required me to retain a master key. My new-found "knight in shining armor," Michael, had been staying in my apartment while I was on a trip. Unknowingly to me, he had duplicated my master key. A few days after I returned from my trip, I was awakened around 4 a.m. to a very bloody scene. A woman was attacked in her bed. She had crawled from door to door leaving a bloody trail behind her, trying to get help, and seeing her blood all over the walls and ceiling, from door to door, utterly devastated me. I went to visit her in the hospital, and she was barely able to open her eyes. It was hard to believe she had survived such a hostile attack. The experience totally shook me, and I went over to my new boyfriend's house to tell him about it, with no clue he had been the perpetrator! One of the detectives had said something about hairy arms, which made me think of

Michael, because I had just been thinking a few days earlier about how hairy his arms were, but I totally discounted that it could have been him.

We ended up moving into a house together, and I went to work for a health food store. One night while at work in the health food store, I got a call from my childhood friend's uncle, Ron. He had been like an uncle to me, too. He was a psychologist for a large corporation, and had written college psychology textbooks. I idolized him as a young teenager. His influence in my life caused me to believe I could find answers in psychology. I subscribed to *Psychology Today*, and other magazines that were similar. As Isaiah the Prophet put it, "Woe to them that go down to Egypt for help..." (Isaiah 31:1). That's where Ron went, and I followed in his footsteps. The help Ron got from Egypt, ended with a shocking tragedy.

Ron called to invite me to his home. I called Michael to tell him I would be going to see him across town and he said the snowfall was very heavy, and the roads were hazardous. He said that I should visit another time, so I didn't go. A few evenings later as Michael and I were watching the evening news, we were horrified to learn what Ron's plans were that snowy evening. He had invited not only me, but my friend Lori, and Ron's three children. His son was the only one who showed up. He was quite larger than Ron, but Ron managed to beat his son to death with a lamp. He then drove to Las Vegas, got into the bathtub, slit his wrists and committed suicide.

Incidents like these often make me wonder how many times the angels of God have guarded and protected us. I'm sure we'll all be shocked to see how busy we have kept them. I used to stroll around parks at night, lost, lonely and confused. These were parks where women are raped and murdered on a regular basis. I was afraid of things I shouldn't have been, and not afraid of things I should have been.

After four months of living with Michael, we married. We had the permission of the state, and the Catholic and Episcopal churches, who both gave us premarital counseling! Too bad they never suggested we turn from our godless, independent ways. They never even suggested we were serving ourselves, not Jesus. The words "sin and fornication" weren't mentioned. We were happy doing our own thing, and we thought it made Jesus happy, too. We cared little about Jesus anyway back then. We were doing our own thing and just expected God to put His stamp of approval on it, just as the state and church did. We never consulted with the inventor and ordainer of marriage. We were doing our own thing our own way. The church and state blessed us, and sent us on our way.

Neither Michael or I were facing the truth about ourselves. We watched soap operas and night sit-coms to avoid our life's problems. We lived life deceiving and being deceived. Looking back, I knew something was wrong, but I had no idea what it felt like to live in honest, open relationships. We didn't see how wrong it was to live life without a relationship with the One who created us — the One who has the blueprint to help us fulfill the master plan of our life. I was unfamiliar with the still, small voice of God's Holy Spirit. I ignored what I knew to be right by joining myself and submitting to a man of deceit. I obeyed my senses and lust, and selfish desires, and I reaped it in the relationship I chose. God was not mocked; what I sowed is what I reaped. It took years for me to see my ways were not God's ways; I was sowing to my flesh, and reaping corruption. I know now I have to sow to the Spirit, to reap life in Jesus.

Two months into my marriage, I became pregnant with our first daughter. Two weeks before my due date I had a dream Michael had killed someone. In horror I woke up so distressed I went into labor. He had come home late from work with his pants wet. He was drunk. I remembered as I folded clothes and watched the evening news, that a story came on about a girl being raped and murdered close by. It never dawned on me that was why he had come home with wet pants. I remember feeling afraid that someone in our neighborhood was murdered. Little did I know I was living with the murderer. I knew he was mean and lied, and drank too much. I called myself married, but felt so alone. I vowed "until death do we part," but I couldn't attach to him because of his dark, secret life. I had never really had anyone to attach to before; that loneliness that always haunted me was still ever present. I had my own compulsive problems and my own destructive comforts.

There were things I turned to because I didn't know the peace and comfort of God — mainly overeating. I joined Overeaters Anonymous. I remember coming face to face with my bad attitudes about God, and I blurted out a prayer: "God, if you're real, please show me." The next few months I started having a perception of evil. I could sense the darkness around me as never before.

I visited a neighborhood church. Many of the women were involved in Alcoholics Anonymous. I began thinking Michael might be an alcoholic. He was always lying, drinking, and he had a definite dark force around him. I ended up leaving him to help him face his problem. Two weeks later, he came to talk to me. He confessed his drinking problem along with criminal offenses he was responsible for. He told me about the infidelities he had committed. Late into the night, he told me he had done things God could not forgive him for. I asked, "Well, what did you do, kill someone?" In his silence and failure to respond, he was sending me a loud message.

Yes, he had killed someone. I quietly left the room. My body was shaking and trembling. For the first time in my life I sensed a good whiff of hell. I was seeing the reality of heaven and hell, right before my eyes. I knew then, God was real, the devil was real, there was evil and good and I knew which side of the fence I wanted to be on. I walked and jogged around the neighborhood until the sun came up and I came upon the little church I had been attending. The priests were having an early morning meeting. They saw the horror on my face and sat me down to talk. I told them Michael had confessed to murder, attempted murder, kidnapping, brutal beatings, rape, and a whole string of crimes. I thought I was going to have a heart attack right there. I was three months pregnant and I started having a miscarriage.

We called Michael and had him come over to the church. He evasively confessed his sins. They told him he was an alcoholic, and he should stop drinking. They told him to go and sin no more; his sins were forgiven. Through the years, even though we spoke with many priests, pastors and counselors, none of them ever suggested he turn himself in, or repent to those he had harmed.

We began to faithfully attend Alcoholics Anonymous. We learned about Michael's disease. The truth is his disease was because he was holding the love of sin in his heart, and was demonized. He was given over to demonic spirits by his own will and lustful desires. We prayed regularly, but Psalm 66:18 says, "If I regard iniquity in my heart, the Lord will not hear *me*." I don't think our prayers were going very far. We had surrounded ourselves with people who made many excuses for our sins, because they wanted excuses for their own sins. We got involved with self-improvement Christian programs. I talked to priest after priest, and person after person. I knew we were really missing something, and things weren't right. The still, small voice of God wasn't letting me be content in my false peace.

I rode the bus downtown to the library one day with our nine-month old baby. I looked through old papers, scanned micro film for hours, and could find nothing. Somehow, I thought if I could come up with any specific information about certain crimes, I could go to the authorities. What about the mother of the woman he murdered? It seemed only right that he should tell her he was sorry and had a drinking problem, a disease like Alcoholics Anonymous was telling us he had. I know now calling his sin a disease was a sorry excuse for his lack of love for Jesus. He loved to commit crimes, and loved to think about committing crimes. That's what no one was willing to be honest about. Looking back now, years after the fact, it shocks me to think of all the professionals we consulted, and that no one ever suggested to him he could get relief for his guilty conscience if he would turn himself in. Isaiah 55:7 says, "Let the wicked forsake his way, and the unrighteous man his thoughts: and let him return unto the Lord, and he will have mercy upon him; and to our God, for he will abundantly pardon."

We psychoanalyzed our past. We went to all kinds of therapy and counseling. We were hypnotized, we visualized Jesus, meditated, went through all our past memories pretending and acting out things that didn't really happen. I read many books, and believed he would be all right if he didn't drink. We blamed father, mother, sister, brother, the Catholic church, the nuns, childhood events, anything to shift responsibility towards someone else. We accused others and excused ourselves, and of course *"the devil made me do it"*

64

seemed like the best of excuses. I searched and psychoanalyzed him for years to find answers for why men lust and rape. (They lust and rape because that's what they want to do!) My oldest sister gave me a book called *Inside The Criminal Mind*. That was when the dark things really began coming into the light. Jesus said it's my food to do the will of Him who sent me. I started seeing it was Michael's "food" to commit and think about committing crimes.

We attended church, counseling, and Alcoholics Anonymous regularly. All was looking well on the outside, but deep within there was a big disturbance in the force. We had two more children over the next few years. I was awakened by a loud banging at the door one night when our third child was just a few months old. Michael had a late night job at a convenience store, and I assumed he had just gotten home. I heard him yell at me, "bring me a towel," from the living room. At the door was a young woman who lived across the street. She said she had been raped by a Hispanic man. We called 911, and when the police arrived, she proceeded to tell the account of her attack. I remember feeling numb inside as I sensed the still, small voice of God telling me something was wrong. I couldn't go back to sleep. That morning I went to see one of the priests who had counseled us. I told him I couldn't live with Michael, because every time I heard of a rape, I feared it was him. I came away from my session with the priest's words ringing in my ears, "Why can't you forgive, forget, and move on with things in your life?" I just assumed all was my fault and I was being paranoid over nothing.

We even started getting secular counseling. They could, and should have turned him in, but Michael always had a way of shedding a bad light on me to get the heat off himself. As the days went on, I felt in my heart that Michael had raped the woman across the street. I even went to help her move out of her house and ask her more questions, to see if I could put my suspicions to rest. He was such a good criminal, and did such sneaky things to discredit the crime scene towards looking to him as the criminal — things like wearing size 14 boots when he really wore size 12. The girl he raped said the rapist didn't speak English, so I thought I was just unable to cope with the past. The clergy recommended biofeedback, transcendental meditation and hypnosis to help me deal with my fear and stress. We also had a fire in our home shortly after that, so I put the incident on the "back burner."

Another home, and another baby later, another disturbing incident happened to shake the false peace we lived in. Michael's business partner came over one morning and announced his next door neighbor had been raped. I had noticed Michael lusting after her before. (He had a really sneaky way of moving his eyes around without moving his head). Some women fail to see the messages they give men by the way they dress. Men justify acting like dogs when women dress seductively, not that they are justified. Anyway, deep in my heart, I wondered if Michael had done it. After asking him a few questions, he turned the light on his partner. He told me what a bad problem with lust the guy had, and how he was trying to help him by sharing his testimony with him. I swallowed it hook, line, and sinker. He always knew what to say.

I still felt as if I lived in a prison with him. I asked Jesus to show me what was wrong. I couldn't attach to him. We were indifferent to each other. I had four small children to keep me busy and he was busy with his contracting business. Neither of us had ever been familiar with close, open, honest, accountable relationships in our lives, so it was life as usual.

His actions spoke volumes to me. He said he loved me, but he behaved as if the kids and I weren't there most of the time. We looked like the struggling religious family on the outside, but I knew in my heart something was missing on the inside. One day I told him to tell me the truth, because his actions did anyway. Our marriage was a facade, and our religion together was hypocrisy. He had a form of seeking God to try to pacify me, but he didn't seek the truth out of his own spiritual hunger.

We lived in private little worlds apart from each other, calling ourselves married, with no spirit of marriage. In the church we attended, I learned a crafty way of praying. The underlying message is, *I can control God through my prayers, and He will control you*. It's a very subtle form of witchcraft, and it just about shipwrecked my faith. I recited prayers with the belief that if I filled in a certain person's name on the dotted line, God would be obligated to control them. *If you pray it, God is obligated to yield to your prayer.* I didn't realize that God doesn't work through control and manipulation because of prayer. He does however, work through influence and persuasion. We don't just automatically have authority over people, places, and things because of our prayers. This kind of teaching was very devastating to me.

I thought Jesus didn't love me anymore when He wouldn't "control" Michael into obeying Him. I had a real "Burger King" mentality of Jesus, which was *give me things my way and I'll love and serve You*. I wasn't living for God and His Kingdom, nor Jesus or His followers and purposes. I lived for my thoughts, my ways, my kingdom, and my world, but declared myself to be a Christian. I served the Jesus of my imagination, not the Jesus in the Bible!

A year later a miracle was about to take place. Michael came home with a hurt ankle. I didn't watch much television or read newspapers, so I wasn't aware of an attempted rape that had occurred in our area. The next day, Michael hadn't gone to church with me. I came home to find him crying (which is very unusual for a prideful man). I went to nap for a few minutes and found myself in a half-awake, half-asleep state of dreaming. I saw myself in a big, open field with a wooden cross about ten feet tall in front of me, and many large filled trash bags behind me. I heard a voice say, "Pick up those nails and hammer, and nail those trash bags on that cross."

As I began to nail them on, the cross began to grow. The next thing I knew, I was looking down on the planet earth, floating above it. The cross had outgrown the planet. During some of my darkest hours, I saw how I limited

God through my ignorance and lack of faith. The following day, I went to a women's Christian luncheon, and upon returning home, I found a note on the door from a local sheriff. He called when Michael got home. I just assumed he wanted some contracting work done. Michael proceeded to tell me some off-the-wall story (which most of the time I bought).

This time however, I didn't believe a word he said. I had a sense, that he had hurt someone. Just as Jesus had opened my eyes to "perceive" evil seven years earlier, I perceived Michael was lying! (I had also recently asked Jesus to open my eyes to see.) I believe when we pray in honesty, sincerely with faith regarding ourselves, He will hear our cry. After Michael finished his long, tedious, deceitful story, I looked him straight in the eyes and said, "I'm sorry you haven't gotten the help you need."

He went from being well-composed, to shaking and trembling. He told me that he had a problem, which had nothing to do with me and ran out the door. I went to the neighbor's house. They didn't get the paper, and they had no television. I told the woman I thought Michael had hurt someone. She mentioned receiving a call to pray for a woman who was sunbathing in the nude, and someone had tried to rape her. The man fled when the woman cried out "Jesus, help me."

When she said the assailant had jumped off a cliff and ran off, I put two and two together, about why Michael had come home limping. After speaking with my friends, we decided to call the police. I was in a state of total shock. It's not every day, well maybe it does happen frequently, that a woman picks up the phone to end her life as she knows it, and to turn her husband in. It was hard for me to believe a man would choose to act that way, totally disregarding any love or respect for his wife and children.

I was panic stricken with fear. The world as I knew it had just come crashing down, and I had little faith Jesus could help me pick up the pieces. Michael came back home. I was ready to give up the "he has a disease" philosophy. The "devil made him do it" seemed a bit too evasive to swallow anymore. He was making bad choices, and we had tried all kinds of "therapies," and he was still choosing to make bad choices. Psalms 4:16-17 says, "For they sleep not, except they have done mischief; and their sleep is taken away, unless they cause some to fall. For they eat the bread of wickedness, and drink the wine of violence."

I tried everything but turning him in. I was advised for years I didn't have enough information, but nothing had successfully stopped him from hurting others. I knew he needed to be stopped, no matter what the cost. I knew my life would be in danger for calling the police, but I didn't care. The Lord put a resolve in my heart that I was not going to allow anyone to cause me to deny any longer. He walked in the house, took one look at me, and he knew what I had done. He read me like a book, and the spirit of "murder" was glaring in his eyes.

He had a wicked way of staying in control of me. There was an eerie silent voice that screamed, *Do what I say, don't cross my will or I'll kill you.* You couldn't hear the words, but you could feel them in the air. I said to Michael, "If you loved me and you had done all you could to help me stop hurting people, and I didn't stop, what would you do?" He stared at me with his murderous eyes, while I prayed silently for Jesus to protect the kids and me. I knew he was very unstable, and he ran out of the house in a rage. I knew an emotional volcano was about to erupt.

I wasn't sure where he was going or what he would do, but I knew a miracle had taken place. Jesus promises to bring the hidden things of darkness to the light. He said there is nothing hidden that will not be revealed. For the first time since meeting Michael, I saw clearly his deceit and wickedness. I saw it was his "food" to do evil. This event began some of the darkest hours of my life. I took our four small children, and left to go stay at my mom's house. I was tormented. Where was he? What was he doing? Would he come and take the kids? Would he kill me for turning him in?

After five days of not eating, and little sleep, Michael called on the phone. I asked him about the woman that lived next to his business partner. He confessed to being the one who had raped her. I asked him about the girl who lived across the street who had been raped a couple of years earlier, and he admitted he was responsible for that, too. All I could say to him is "Do what you have never done: tell the truth; maybe it will set you free."

He decided to turn himself in, but controlled and manipulated the whole thing, his usual style. He had the sheriff, pastor, a lawyer from the church and me, meet him in a park by our home. The lawyer brought a colleague and together they advised him not to confess, but try to work out a plea bargain. The pastor had no opinion, but the Sheriff and I were indignant. That "still, small voice" was telling me, *this is not true repentance.*

The Sheriff's Department didn't have enough evidence to hold him, in spite of all I had told them about. I realized why all the past counselors had advised against me turning him in. The hard reality of prosecuting a criminal today is they just about have to commit the crime on the doorstep of the Police Department to be prosecuted and convicted.

Michael's brother drove across the state to see if he could help, when he heard what was going on. His only, and older brother, treats sexual offenders for a living. He employs physiologists in his clinic that treats the sexual offenders in a big metropolis city. He travels the country giving seminars on how to treat sexual offenders, and has been doing this all the years his brother has been a sexual offender! His comment to Michael was, "I can't believe you would hurt a fly."

There are so many things I could tell about the shocking details of this story. To tell it all would truly take a book. I still marvel that my children and I lived through it, and I know God sent ministering angels to help us. I know without Jesus in my life and the power of His Holy Spirit, I would have ended up in an insane asylum, dying of self-pity.

For the next few months, I lived life on the run like an animal being hunted. We stayed in shelters. I stayed in a friend's vacated house. He was like a predator who had lost control of his prey. The police were trying to protect me. The stress was tremendous, and it was taking its toll on me. I was an emotional wreck. I was tired, sick, terrified and exhausted. My days were filled with panic and terror, wondering if he would "catch" the kids and me.

I ended up going to stay with the mother of my childhood best friend. She was in great fear for our lives, and invited us to hide out in her home. We began to talk, and she thought the information she had about a murder Michael had committed, varied from the information I had. I began wondering if there was a discrepancy in the information I had given the Sheriff's Department months earlier.

I began calling the different county authorities where I thought he had committed rapes, kidnappings, and attempted murder. The regular investigator was on vacation. The man I spoke with "miraculously" happened to be going through old files — which they rarely ever do! As I spoke, he said, "I'm driving across town right now to come and see you." He did, and he had a drawing by the police artist through a description of a woman Michael had kidnapped, raped, and tried to murder. It looked just like him. They had fingerprints, and thought they may be able to arrest him.

I called another county where I thought a murder had taken place. The detective went downstairs to the archives and dug up a file of an old murder. After he looked at the file he stated, "You wouldn't know the details you know, if you hadn't talked to the murderer." Both of the detectives looked shocked and bewildered that they had not received more information from the county that I had originally given details to months earlier. I was horrified. Why were these counties withholding critical information from each other? Why were they allowing a murderer to be on the loose and failing to communicate vital information? Were they in some kind of competition to catch him first?

It became apparent to me that I was going to have to stay personally involved if Michael was to be arrested and brought to justice. The investigators questioned why I hadn't come forth at an earlier date. I had to admit that, because of advice given to me in the past by many church officials and leaders, I wouldn't make a judgment that agreed with my own conscience. Even counselors that didn't vow to silence because of priestly vows, didn't go to the officials.

In all the multitudes of friends and church members I spoke with over the years, no one ever suggested to give information I knew about Michael to the authorities. I began to see how terrible the church's position on "not making a judgment" really is. In fact, Jesus said in John 7:24, "Judge not according to the appearance, but judge righteous judgment." Looking back on it now — and remembering all the people I spoke with who have great influence and authority over people's lives, and failed to see the violation of conscience Michael lived in — scares me.

How could he even think of knowing forgiveness when he failed to go to those he offended? There was a responsibility he needed to fulfill. A decency and order in taking responsibility for what he had done. I always asked the question, "What about the mothers who have lost daughters?" Shouldn't Michael at least let them know he was an alcoholic and has stopped drinking and was sorry. No one could ever answer that, and I knew in my heart that wasn't right.

The truth is he loved to use women, control them, and gratify his lust regardless of who got hurt. Everyone was willing to excuse his behavior because of alcohol. The disease, was a scapegoat for sin. Looking back on our church experiences, we never met a man who had taken the log of lust from his own eye, so he could see clearly what to do with Michael. *(At least no one who was willing to come clean with their own lust problem).*

What man growing up in this day and age, could possibly escape life without having to deal with lust? When you excuse your own wrong behavior, you're more than willing to excuse the wrong behavior of others, not help them face the truth and do what's right. I have come to love the judgment Jesus talks about! The Bible says God loves judgment and we will be saved by judgment! Psalm 119:92 says, "Unless thy law *had been* my delights, I should then have perished in mine affliction." Jesus judged the robbers in His Father's house. He whipped them and threw them out! He continually judged people's problems, and by telling them, He gave them the cure.

I had the feeling that the detectives would have been indignant towards my apathy, had it not been for their own organizational incompetence in transferring the information I had given months earlier. I never did get an answer why there had been such a gross failure to communicate information between counties. Michael could have been arrested months earlier.

There was a serial murderer and rapist loose in Denver during the time I found him out. When he was actually arrested, God only knows what criminal behavior he was up to in those months. I consider it a miracle that I stayed with my friend's mother. She provoked me to call and discover critical information that had been withheld. This event did lead to his arrest weeks later. Who knows how long the system would have taken, or if he ever would have been apprehended and convicted without one phone call, and without making a judgment and following through with it.

Hopeless and despairing, my mom had no idea what to do with me. I was on drugs for depression, and was sick and melting away from stress and lack of sleep. I was falling off the deep end of hopelessness, and flipping out. My mom took me across the state to an Adult Children Of Alcoholics Clinic run by a priest she knew from her past. After I was there two weeks, they told me I needed to leave, because I was endangering the lives of others if Michael showed up.

I packed up the kids and me in the morning and right before I left, a detective called. They wanted my help to find Michael and arrest him. They told me to make a plan to meet him somewhere, and instead of me being there, they would show up and capture him. I suggested his parent's home. Then I called and left messages with people we knew. He called me back and I arranged to meet him. I went to the city with the kids and rented a motel room until they called me to inform me they had apprehended him.

I was nervous all night and feared Michael might recognize the car, because the motel was right off the highway. I tried to hide it the best I could. I cried with relief upon receiving a call the next day — they had broken the door down and had him in custody. They staked out the neighborhood, which I'm sure was terrifying to the whole neighborhood. I knew it was questionable how long they could hold him, or if his relatives would help him make bail.

Everything was resting on his willingness to confess. My relief was short lived when I received a call from the authorities that he was not cooperating. When he called me from jail, I told him I didn't have the strength to take care of the kids and myself, and I wasn't going to speak to him again unless he made a full confession. He had already spent thousands of the taxpayer's dollars with his manipulation and control.

I started thinking, *If I had murdered and done the things he had, I would say, 'I'm sorry and I'm worthy of death,' and let the chips fall where they may.* I knew he wasn't really sorry. He was sorry for himself, and he still didn't care about pleasing God. I wasn't willing to be his conscience anymore. He ended up making a full confession the next day, but only to stay in control of the kids and me. It was my requirement, and he had fulfilled it, not because of his convictions, but mine. I was seeing how truly sick our relationship was, and always had been.

Though he was locked up, I was tormented with the possibility of him making bail. The state had let him go after a psychological evaluation before his arrest. They said he showed no signs of mental or emotional disturbance. They were trying to prove him insane. They wouldn't let him confess. They were trying to protect him and get him off the hook. It was insane!

Friends and relatives helped with my kids. The stress was just about unbearable. Life didn't seem worth living. How could we ever outlive the effects of the father-husband murderer? Aren't the sins of the fathers passed onto the children? What hope would my children have? I was traumatized, and they were traumatized. I felt dead inside, and was terrified they might still let him go.

My sister offered to take care of my baby for awhile. I thought they would all be better off without me and without the remembrance of Michael and me. Too bad they weren't all babies and could put this nightmare behind them. Michael had terrorized our oldest daughter and her teacher by kidnapping her from school and trying to drive her across the state line. He turned around when he realized he was being followed and couldn't escape with her.

I considered the power of words, the song of my heart. You see, when I was nine years old, I learned to sing and play the guitar. The first song I learned was about a railroad boy who forsook his girl. She hung herself to death. I sang the song over and over as a kid. Now, the man of my dreams had forsaken me and I'm left suicidal. The song of my childhood came true. The power music has in lives can be devastating. I needed Jesus to put a new song in my heart.

Nine months later as I was returning from a Christian retreat, my car broke down. I ended up very near to where Michael was being held and sentenced for murder. I felt God's destiny in my going to the hearing, and after what happened, I knew it was. As I sat in the courtroom, watching some of Michael's victims come in, one girl in particular with a long scar across her neck, I didn't think I could handle it.

I went downstairs to a cafeteria, unable to control my tears. A young police officer addressed me, and asked if he could help me. I told him the circumstances of why I was there, and he told me what circumstances had brought him there. He was the family representative for his niece whom Michael had murdered. Her 13 brothers and sisters were too enraged to come. I was shocked as the realization hit me: I was standing in front of the uncle of one of Michael's dead victims! This was a sobering sad reality of lost life.

He was kind as he took me back upstairs. The bailiff addressed me and told me the judge and Michael wanted to see me. Michael was losing his nerve to confess. I realized why I was there, and I began to preach to Michael regarding confessing as the right and only thing to do, and I was indignant in my position. I told him it wasn't right to put conditions on the consequences and he should accept them, come what may if he was truly sorry.

Well, against the advice of his counsel, and the pressure of my being there, his attorney pleads guilty. He went on to give all the reasons why Michael was a good criminal and should be rewarded for his honorable behavior. The judge then delivered a powerful, anointed address to the courtroom. He said, "Woe unto us the day we reward criminals for doing what is right, and their obligation to do in merely confessing and owning up to their crimes."

After all the sentencing was over, Michael received 150 years. He would be a free man today had he not confessed. He never has faced responsibility for many of the crimes he committed, because of the statute of limitations. Detectives from 10 counties met to discuss the possibility of solving murders Michael could be linked to. I received two phone calls saying they would give him amnesty if he would confess to the murders they thought he was responsible for. I doubt I will ever fully know the extent of the "private life" he led apart from me in our time together.

I was beginning to face the multitude of bad counsel I had received from religious leaders. Michael was begging me from prison to "do things his way." I knew in my heart, I was his umbilical cord to his God-conscience, and the cord must be cut. Wasn't divorce the unpardonable sin? The Bible says in Mark 10:9, "What therefore God hath joined together, let not man put asunder." The downright truth was, God never joined us together! Our sin, compromise, and selfishness joined us. God had nothing to do with it, and we had lived a life apart from Jesus. His Spirit, the Spirit of Truth, hadn't been a part of our union, and that's why we could never truly be joined.

I finally became willing to call dead something that had never lived (our relationship)! I got the feeling from the religious circles we were in, that I was committing a sin greater than murder. The truth is, Michael had always been joined to his love of crime. The spirit of divorce was always alive and well in our relationship, long before we got a paper from the state to validate the fact.

We had lived in a state of divorce from the day we were supposedly married. Michael was irate, because he would lose points, and privilege with the prison board if I were to leave him. I had been taking the children to jail to see him and it was devastating them. They only knew the Dr. Jekyll Dad, not Mr. Hyde. I didn't know what to do about taking the kids to see him. The church was telling me I needed to love him unconditionally, but I wasn't sure I was doing the right thing for my kids.

Pride was something Michael and I had discussed time and again. I knew he continually lied to me to present a false front. He always lied to protect his pride, and God is never mocked. What you sow is what you will reap. Every tree will eventually bear fruit for all to see.

Watching Michael's face on television continually, and in the newspapers, caused great shame to come upon me. For a year and a half, I went to bed wanting to die, and woke up in the same condition. I believed we could never outlive the reproach that had come upon us. I hid in a lonely world of depression thinking no one, not even Jesus could understand. The door of my heart was wide open for destruction and despair to come in, and in they did come.

I remember watching the movie *The Never Ending Story* with the kids. The Big Nothing was destroying the land. That's what was destroying me! I had daydreams of how much better we might be if we departed from this world. The baby was gone; she was staying with my sister, and would never remember Michael, and the horrors we were living through.

I went to church and was pitied, and found I was feeling increasingly sorry for myself and depressed when I left. The Bible says in Proverbs 29:18, "Where there is no vision, the people perish..." No one had any understanding to help me. I knew I could spend a lifetime with people pitying me, and it didn't seem too appealing. I had come to realize that many times, those who pity you will end up despising you. The life of Jesus isn't in your soul, when you bring your life to have others pity you!! Feeling sorry for myself and the kids was killing me. Focusing on me, myself and I, and my fear, was tormenting to say the least.

I was realizing I didn't really know the Lord of my faith, and that the only kingdom I understood was man's kingdom. My world of fear, doubt, and unbelief was crashing down on me. I remember thinking my life was one pile of dung. What good could possibly come from it? I heard that still, small voice in my head say, "I use... to make fertile ground!"

Since I've gotten to know Gene, I have come to know much more of Jesus, and Jesus has used Gene to bring His spirit of deliverance into my life. I was at a point where I was ready to face the truth about my hypocrisies — truth I had covered up with too much television.

Gene is anything but pretentious, and pretenders don't hang around him too long. There is nothing hidden or private about his life. Those who are hidden and private don't hang around very long. I was like a drug addict going through withdrawals as I got to know him. He didn't torment, abuse, or reject me. It was unfamiliar and unusual having a man respond to me spiritually, and I could see there was something in me that was uncomfortable not being used, abused, rejected and controlled.

He suffered me as I worked through these things. He was honest and loved me freely, and I was like an old computer having to receive new information. He wasn't emotionally and spiritually unavailable. He lived to give the Lord and himself to others, not to see what he could take in relationships. He helped me and others care about pleasing God in all we think, do and say.

The lifetime of fear I lived in was turning into a lifetime of faith. He had as much passion for faith, love and truth, as Michael had for crime and evil. Michael ate the bread of wickedness, drank the wine of violence, and didn't sleep until he did evil. It was Gene's food to do God's will and he gave that food to all around him. He took on responsibility in relationships, where most men run from it. I watched him give himself to other men. He had answers and understanding, and was willing to have enough love and faith to get personally involved in people's lives. I only knew impersonal Sunday and Wednesday preachers.

I found myself wanting to find things to accuse him of so I could run from the relationship. It took faith to get involved, and that was one thing I didn't have much faith in Jesus for... getting personal in relationships. How could I say I loved God whom I didn't see, if I couldn't love this man whom I did see? I wasn't familiar with open and honest relationships. The more open I became, the more I could see who was "hiding."

I understood how flattery works great ruin in relationships. I had looked to Jesus in faith for things, but now I needed him to give me faith to be honest about the judgments I was making in my heart. I needed faith to not be pretentious and tell the truth. The Bible is full of "put away lying and speak the truth to one another in love" messages.

I began taking those words seriously, believing we are members of each other. Cells that communicate falsely, or indifferently in our body, cause cancer. I decided to be a life-giving cell, rather than a cancerous cell, in the body of Christ. I really began to take the "logs" from my own eyes, so I could see clearly to help remove the specks from the eyes of my friends.

A few months after I had gotten to know Gene, we both knew the Lord had caused our paths to cross for a reason. We got down on our knees and asked the Lord to confirm our relationship, by the mouth of two or three witnesses. We wanted others to confirm that we belonged together, and we knew we could trust Him to open the eyes of others if we were to be together.

Within the span of a week, that's exactly what happened. We courted for a year, then we married. Gene's rule over his flesh did a lot to show me the power and love of God. I knew Gene cared more for pleasing the Lord than gratifying his desires, and I know I can trust him. We have been married 12 years now, and his love continues to reveal God's love and faithfulness to me.

His ability to rule himself before our wedding has proven to me his trustworthiness when we are apart. He chose pleasing Jesus above serving his flesh, and the spirit he carries he imparts to others. The fruit of Jesus' spirit is self-control. As athletes need training, me and many like me are thankful to Jesus for sending us a "personal trainer," who can teach us the ways of "self-control." Many throughout history have been destroyed through uncontrolled lust. How many never accessed the help that was right in front of their face because of pride?

One of Gene's closest friends shared his testimony about how he loved to lust after women. I had never really heard men be open and honest like that. He said, "What I loved, is what Jesus hated; I asked Him to help me love what He loves and hate what He hates." I remember feeling short-circuited. Could it be that simple: Repent and believe Jesus can help you?

He said he confessed his sins, and people prayed for him, and Jesus healed him. I thought to myself, *After all the books, counseling, money we've spent, wouldn't it be hysterical if it was that simple?* I saw this man, along with Gene and other men, have enough humility to be honest and open. I realized Michael's biggest problem was pride! Jesus hates pride above all things!

Michael always lied to protect his pride; that's why he could never get helped! He couldn't even get help from his own brother who had been treating sexual offenders all the years Michael had been sexually offending! If it's true that "For there is nothing hid, which shall not be manifested; neither was any thing kept secret, but that it should come abroad." (Mark 4:22), then I absolutely declared I wouldn't hide anything ever again. I saw what killing your pride by telling the truth had done for these men, and I wanted what they had! (I wanted peace and confidence before Jesus and men).

They believed because they loved the praise of God more than the praise of men, and they had no fear of being condemned by men. The only way to know if Jesus' Words are true is to do them. That's why they knew the Words of Jesus were true. They did them! This was way too simple for a complicated mind like mine!?

I had mentioned earlier that my baby daughter had gone to be with my sister. When I was confident that Michael's sentence was not subject to appeal and after I was recovered from the ordeal, we would make arrangements for the baby's return. My sister knew I was unstable and wanted to help me not make any unwise decisions during a time of crisis. My baby girl was sixteen months old at the time she went to stay with my sister. Michael's actual sentencing was almost one year later.

I met Gene just after the sentencing and one year later, we were married. During this period I saw my little girl only about four times because of my sister's location being on the east coast. My mindset at this time was still very doubtful. It's hard to explain, but even though Jesus was using Gene to bring me great hope and give me vision and direction, I was still thinking that this was not really going to last. Any day something will come up and I will once again be on my own.

At this point I would like to go back to something that happened the night after I met Gene at the concert. I had a dream, and in the dream I was in my bathroom getting ready for the day, when I noticed a rank odor with a stench that made me believe something dead was in there. I looked up, and high up attached to the ceiling was a "body bag" with Michael inside. He had been dead a long time. The thought came to me that I needed to call the men in white suits to come and get him. Three men in white shirts came and got the body bag down and took him away. The eerie thing is that the phone then rang and it was Michael calling from the prison. I wondered if God was trying to show me Michael's conscience was dead towards Him, and I was "dragging a dead body around."

When I went to breakfast later that morning, I thought it was ironic that Gene and the two men with him all had on white ministry t-shirts. I did not remember this or put it together until a couple of weeks later, after the church incident where the Lord healed my ears and also where I had spilled the coffee on myself. I had the three of them over for dinner. After dinner I went to my cabinet and drug out all the newspaper articles about Michael and his life of crime which I had faithfully been saving from day one!

Gene spoke to me about how it was keeping me spiritually attached to Michael and the utter reproach of being his wife. He told me that if I were to ever be free, I would need to completely put off the old and allow "all things" to be made new! He helped me to see that thoughts are words and words are food. The food we eat (what we allow ourselves to think) is what we will become and how we will be in our spirit and in our character. I would say that this was the beginning of my walk away from a life of bondage and trying to fix myself into the freedom and life of letting go.

That night I gathered everything that had to do with Michael, our past and every picture and article. I put it all in a garbage bag and Gene took it away with him and the guys when they left. The three men in white ministry t-shirts had come and taken away the stinking dead body of the past. I could now start over. All my life growing up and throughout my married life, I considered the counseling and counselors: psychologists, doctors, priests, family, friends, and in-laws; no one ever reflected to me the simplest and most fundamental thing I must first do: "Put out the offender"... stop living with your tormentors. The fundamental words of the Master are in Mark 8:35, "For whosoever will save his life shall lose it; but whosoever shall lose his life for my sake and the gospel's, the same shall save it."

So let us go back to one year after Michael's sentencing when Gene and I married. I had said that my mindset was one of doubt, that any day now everything would fall apart. Although I was truly free from Michael, I was not at all free from my foundational enemy, "Rejection!" There is a Scripture in Jeremiah 17:1 which says, "The sin of Judah is written with a pen of iron, *and* with the point of a diamond: *it is* graven upon the table of their heart..." This is exactly what rejection throughout my lifetime had done to me. Rejection was deeply engraved in my soul.

I heard, saw, and responded to most people out of the engraved spirit of rejection in my heart. I always felt like there was something that I needed to do for people so that they would not reject me. I believed it was my responsibility to prove myself in all relationships, and failed to see the responsibility of others. I don't think Michael had people in his life hold him responsible, and I knew it was a tragedy that he believed life didn't have consequences.

It created great fear and doubt in me toward others also, because I never thought that I could ultimately do enough in the relationship to keep it free from offense. This created skepticism and control in me toward those who were closest. I was so afraid of being rejected, I would create scenarios to get Gene to reject me. I didn't believe he could love me. I would many times "third-degree" him when he was out during the day, thinking that he would end up being as unfaithful to me as Michael was.

I'll never forget the look on his face and what he said to me when the Lord opened his understanding to my accusations and fears. He said, "I am willing to prove my love and faithfulness to you by logging my time and meetings. I'll tell you who I've seen, what was said, how long it took and where I went next if it will help you to know that I love you and will never be unfaithful!" I broke down crying for quite some time. This was a man who ran into responsibility, not away from it. He was willing to prove his love. I realized this was a man who knew and looked to Jesus. He responded to my problems spiritually, not carnally. It was making the difference between hell on earth, and heaven on earth in my soul.

My mother had come to our wedding and had gone out with Gene and I once or twice to talk with us after we were married. I felt like her concerns were just a mom being normal, but Gene was uncomfortable with her pretense. It was something I grew up with and was totally familiar with and didn't see at first. The day came soon enough when my family's hidden agenda would be clearly seen.

Everything up to this point was hidden. I had not asked my sister to bring my daughter back and she had not offered. Nothing was spoken about it. One day Gene began to draw me out about my feelings in getting her back. It was like listening to someone else talk. I could not give a clear sound. Inside I wanted her back. Outside I knew that my sister did not want to give her up and I didn't want to cause her pain. I also did not want to face the family feud which I knew would ensue.

To Gene it was without question that she should come back. She is your daughter. The only reason that your sister has her now is because of your having to run from a murderous husband and to give you aid in time of peril. Your peril is over. But, your sister loves your baby and it wouldn't be right to just go ask for her back, but we definitely need to go speak with her. He saw the other children were devastated by her absence.

Gene and I flew to the east coast to talk to my sister personally about the situation. We sat up late with her and we poured out our hearts to each other. She knew my pain and I saw hers. She had her own revelation that the baby should come be with us. I broke down hysterically with unbelievable joy — she was offering my baby back. We didn't have to ask for her, she saw it was the right to restore our family after the storm had passed. My sister admitted that she knew in her heart if we thought the baby belonged with us, we should leave with her in the morning. Her time was over as a guardian angel who had kept a baby safe in a nightmare. She saw it was right for the other children.

When we got up the next morning, my sister was gone and had taken the baby with her. She had gone to get a court order against us. She and my mom had accused me of being an unfit mother, although they weren't trying to have the other children removed from my custody. My sister had money and influence; I didn't even have a lawyer. When you're up against money and power, the battle looked grim. God allowed her to adopt the baby, however. I know the purpose for that has yet to unfold. Even when Social Services did a home study about our family conditions, they recommended the baby be returned to us.

Although I was greatly saddened by my family's betrayal I had understanding and a grace which allowed me to move on and to know that God's purposes would be fulfilled. And basically, what in truth we were dealing with was the persecution of our faith that Jesus talks about.

How strange it was, that through all of Michael's criminal behavior, his drinking and his anger, my family thought me to be normal and would not have considered taking my children away from me or accusing me of being unfit. If

I were unfit at any time in my life it was during the last year of my marriage to Michael. Why weren't they taking me to court back then?

The plain truth is that I had no testimony of Jesus in all that was happening. All I could do was relate to them on a carnal, sensual level. The dead religion we were raised in has no real belief that God is involved personally through His Son Jesus in your life, and that He will actually speak to you in your spirit and give you wisdom and guidance.

Had I been enlightened with the Holy Spirit, and had the people of God come into my life back then, my family would have gone after me. As a child I never understood why the people back in Jesus' day killed him. As I grew older and went to church, it just became fact but I never really understood why people get so threatened by those who have encountered the Living God of the Bible!

Spiritual persecution is merely two people whose spirits are in disagreement or in conflict, and one decides to punish the other or to control the other. And this is what my family was doing. They were using the ignorant and ungodly courts and prejudiced system of law to justify their lies and control. I never was persecuted when I loved and served myself, and could care less about serving Jesus. I let Michael control me, and now I was yielding to the Spirit of the Living God, and they thought I went crazy.

Out of the blue one day, we received a phone call. It was my daughter; she was ten. We were ecstatic, because we had been kept from her for years. She ended up coming to visit us several times, and now lives with us. She sees the emptiness of living for money, education and position in life, and the loneliness and lack of true fulfillment it brings. She sees life without faith and love in it isn't worth living. She is becoming familiar with honest, open, sincere relationships. She has given up trashy music and television programs and feeds her heart and spirit with good things rather than destructive things.

She has value in knowing Jesus — the Way, the Truth and the Life! She was tormented because she violated her God-conscience all the time but now she is getting in touch with following the integrity of God's Spirit in her heart. My mother also within the last year has repented for her unfounded fears and imaginations about Gene and I, and how it affected relationships over the years. We talk on a regular basis and enjoy a relationship in spirit and truth. Love and faith have replaced fear and unbelief. I have a saying I like to quote: "perfect fear, casts out love." There is a fear that isn't good; the fear that keeps us from reaching out and loving someone.

Jesus took twelve men and lived in a close relationship with them. He loved them enough to get very involved in their lives, and to teach them to get very involved in lives. He didn't send them away to Bible college to learn to love their brother. Gene along with other men I know, don't read to men from a pulpit, but they get personally involved in the lives of others! This is not a popular concept for those who feel good and righteous because they went to church on Sunday and Wednesday, but never got too close to anyone, nor let anyone close to them.

When I saw Gene give people his heart, talk openly about the motives and intentions of his heart, and help other's have the faith to face the motive and intentions of their hearts, all I could do was cry. I wondered what would have happened if Michael's father would have given him his heart? What if he was honest with him about his own lust and pretense, would it have made a difference in his life?

I look back on all the priests, counselors, and men in the churches we attended who were not honest and open about overcoming sin in their lives. They didn't have the testimony of Jesus regarding their sin and selfishness. If they did, they loved their own lives too much to talk about it. They weren't open, and they didn't produce openness in Him. They "bore fruit after their own kind."

The love of Jesus in my heart for my children, demanded me to find answers for them. I didn't want them to walk down the path of destruction and perversion that generations in our family had, which I haven't still gone into great depth about. (It would take a book). I don't condemn my family, but I can't close my eyes to reality and deny Jesus with them anymore. I love Jesus, the Light, and most of them don't. "Be ye not unequally yoked together with unbelievers: for what fellowship hath righteousness and unrighteousness? and what communion hath light with darkness?" (II Corinthians 6:14). I love and pray for them, and believe Jesus to send others into their lives they might not reject. I lived in the dark, and Jesus sent His people to me to walk in the Light with them. Now I live to help others (who will let me) walk in the Light with Jesus, the Son of God, who is Light!

Meeting people who didn't hide their sin, but exposed it, has changed my life forever! Consider the movie, *Schindler's List*: One man doing what was right, what love demanded, saved the lives of many. All who have eyes to see the path His life has laid out for us, and receive Him, are saved! I thank God He sent men my way who were doing what was right, what love demands. It's helped me to be the one sent, and to send to others the message of deliverance from the kingdom of darkness, into the Kingdom and Government of God.

In the book of Acts, it shows the Apostle Paul was required to receive Annanias so he could receive his sight. Cornelius also, after being visited by an angel, was instructed to send for a man, Peter. Cornelius received Jesus, because He received Peter. If Cain would have humbled himself to receive his brother Abel, God would have received his offering. His evil heart towards his brother was his ruin. God, throughout history, has ordained men to be messengers of His Word and Grace.

The Bible says, "There was a man sent from God, whose name *was* John." (John 1:6). In my case, his name was Gene. God has always sent men. He promised to! He sent Jesus, and Jesus sent men! Michael chose to be an ambassador of hell and death. Gene chose to be an ambassador of Faith, Hope, Love, and Jesus! We all must choose who we will represent. I want to have the Bread of Life, the drink of heaven, for all who Jesus sends my way.

He's coming back to reward us for what we have done: for what we did about what we thought; for what we said; and how we affected each other, good and bad. Our words are on a mission; they operate on the hearts of those around us. What mission are your words on? What operation do you perform in the lives of those around you? Job 29:12-16 says, "Because I delivered the poor that cried, and the fatherless, and *him that had* none to help him. The blessing of him that was ready to perish came upon me: and I caused the widow's heart to sing for joy. I put on righteousness, and it clothed me: my judgment *was* as a robe and a diadem. I was eyes to the blind, and feet *was* I to the lame. I *was* a father to the poor: and the cause *which* I knew not I searched out."

That's the end of my story, but in actuality it is not the end. My life is just beginning! God's Word says in II Corinthians 5:17, "Therefore if any man *be* in Christ, *he is* a new creature: old things are passed away; behold, all things are become new."

CHAPTER 17

Delivered From Low Self-Esteem and Illicit Sex
The Darrell Anderson Story

God delivered me from low self-esteem and a lack of self-worth which led to an addiction to prostitutes, pornography and illicit sex.

People often look at children who get into trouble and they wonder how they could do such a thing. In some cases, we think they are supposed to be perfect children. They come from a family with two professional parents who make a lot of money; they live in a big home in the suburbs; they attend the best schools; they have a computer, a colored television, every Nintendo game ever made; and some have a fancy car. For most children, the pain or insecurities that cause them to act out (in whatever way they do) began developing much earlier. Most of our families and loved ones love us unconditionally and they see nothing but good things about us. Little do they know the feelings of self-doubt that are growing inside. In America, we too often measure happiness by how much money and material possessions we have and/or how beautiful/ handsome a person is. Kids discover something that adults do not know, have forgotten or do not care to think about. Kids discover that money and looks are not the keys to happiness. Kids are longing for ultimate happiness and they are crying out for help. If kids do not receive adequate love and attention from their parents, or if they are not introduced to God or refuse to accept God, they will go searching for that happiness in all the wrong places.

I do not come from a well-to-do family, but like those children, the self-doubt and lack of self-worth started growing in me at an early age. Because I stayed in school, got good grades, stayed in church, and took care of my sick mother, I appeared to be a perfect child and nobody knew the inner conflict. My mother started having nervous breakdowns when I was ten years old. My father was shot and killed when my mother was two months pregnant with me. She already had five kids. She had another child after me. The pressure from raising seven children by herself and losing her home, caused the nervous breakdowns. As a result of my mother's illness, some of my siblings turned to drugs to deal with the pain. Others were totally indifferent. I was always told that I was the smartest one in the family. Therefore, believing that, I felt obligated to take care of my mother and try to keep the family together. Before this happened, I was already very shy and quiet. I had no confidence and a very low self-esteem. Even though I made the grade at school, I could not get to first base on a personal level. Thus, once I became everybody's hero and the one everybody looks up to, I withdrew inward. I became a recluse. I spent so much time being an adult in a child's body that I lost the ability to relate to people my own age. I did not know how to communicate with girls.

One night in April 1984, I was walking home. I was only 16 years old and a virgin. I saw a prostitute standing on a corner. The devil told me, *You better get her because that is the only way you will ever get a woman.* I agreed with him and I believed that lie for the next 13 1/2 years. I paid that prostitute to have sex with me. These women did not require me to talk to them, to open up my heart and share who I really was with them. Whenever I would meet a girl who was bold enough to make the first move, I would assume that she would not like me once she got to know the real me. It was easier for me to pay a prostitute and not have to face possible rejection. Thus, I could continue to hide and not deal with these issues. When people first get into the world of pornography and illicit sex, the devil can make it seem so exciting. You get to experiment with many different kinds of people. You can fulfill any kind of fantasy you can think of. If one person will not perform the act, there is always another. The only question for me was whether I had the money to pay. When a sexual encounter with one woman was no longer satisfying, I turned to couples. These wives and girlfriends were beautiful, decent, clean, respectable, intelligent and I did not have to pay. Thus, after such experiences, you might think I would feel like I was walking on air. Nevertheless, I felt even worse.

The devil does not tell people about the consequences of this kind of behavior. This kind of lifestyle severely damaged my emotions, my whole perspective on life, and my ability to give myself to one person. Even those women who choose to do it for themselves and not for a pimp or boyfriend feel the same effects. They reach a point in which they are sick and tired of this lifestyle but they feel trapped. I got to the point in which I thought I was nothing. I felt like I was lower than the dirt that people walk on everyday. That was how I treated myself and that was how I expected others to treat me.

I was arrested for the first time in June 1994, on O'Farrell Street, a main street in one of the red-light districts in San Francisco. I had never been arrested before, so I got off easy. I was allowed to participate in pretrial diversion and the charges were dismissed. I did not heed the warning. Instead, I thought that I should just be more careful about who I select to solicit. In December 1996, I was arrested again on Capp Street between 17th and 18th Streets. Capp Street is another popular street in one of the red-light districts in San Francisco. This time I had to hire a really good lawyer to fight for me. At first I still did not see the need to change. But during the months of plea bargaining, the Lord got my attention and told me this is the last time I will get off easy, so I better get my act together. The charges were reduced to "breach of the peace" and I was awarded pretrial diversion again and counseling. Upon completion of diversion and counseling, the charges were dismissed. I did not feel like I wanted to be saved, but I knew the Lord was calling me and I was miserable. So in April 1997, I stood up in front of the whole congregation and repented; then, I was baptized in Jesus' Name. However, I did not fully commit myself. I did not allow God to fill me with His Spirit (the Holy Ghost). Therefore, I had nothing to fight the devil with when he came back to tempt me to pick up prostitutes again.

Part of my plea bargain agreement required me to take counseling. Ironically, there was a counselor who just started his job the same week I started attending the group counseling sessions. This counselor had the same problem I had when he was younger. However, he treated my problem from a carnal-minded point-of-view only. He felt that all I needed was to have one good experience with one decent woman who really liked me for who I am. His talks helped me to recognize that I did have a problem. He also helped me to feel a little better about myself temporarily. However at the same time, I knew that his advice was not reaching deep enough.

A friend at work offered to introduce me to a friend of his girlfriend. I had never done anything like this before. I knew right away that this relationship was not right, but I was excited by the opportunity to date someone who I thought really liked me and date her the normal way. I also figured this would be a good opportunity to experiment with some of the things I was told by the counselor. To make a long story short, the relationship was a disaster because I still had those issues to deal with. As a result of the failed attempt at a relationship, I went back to the streets.

On November 20, 1997, it happened again. I was arrested for solicitation on 18th and Capp Streets. When I saw the police lights flashing this time, the only thing I could say is *"Oh God, you warned me."* I knew I could not run anymore because God would keep running me into brick walls. I spent the next three weeks trying to get myself in the mindset to give my life to Christ because I knew that He was the only one who could break me from this terrible habit. On December 14, 1997, I was baptized again. Four days later, I received the Holy Ghost. Once Christ came into my life, I had the power to resist the temptations of the devil. I have found what I and everyone else longs for: ultimate happiness, inner peace, and freedom. God has shown me who I am and what my purpose in life is. He has taught me how to love myself, how to respect myself, how to take care of myself, how to treat a woman, and how to give myself to my future wife. I have not attempted to be intimate with anyone since November 20, 1997 and I do not plan to be intimate with anyone until the night of my wedding. I am content to wait until God allows me to meet the wife that He has prepared for me.

From the moment Christ came into my life, I knew I had been delivered and I immediately felt a need to go back to the red-light districts and let people know that there is hope. I know there is hope because I found the answer. In March 1999, God called me to the ministry and told me to do just that. In May 1999, I finally got the courage to walk down the same streets where I used to go to pick up women. I talk to women I used to know, women I have never met, pimps, drug addicts, drug dealers, and anyone else who will listen. I talk to them about God's power to deliver them and heal them. I share my testimony with them to let them know that I can identify with them. Then I explain to them how God has changed my life. I feed them if they are hungry. On occasion, I have provided shelter. I realize that their problems run so deep that it is important to build a relationship with them. They are so afraid of leaving the abusive relationships or situations they are in because they are afraid that they will be alone and not have anyone to love them. It is my job to be a living example for them; to show them that they can be happy with Jesus alone.

Even though God is powerful enough to save anyone in an instant, it usually does not happen that way. There is a cleansing process that a person has to go through. Oftentimes when a person is suffering, that person can feel that he/she is the only one in the world who is feeling this type of pain and thus nobody would understand. I truly believe that if someone like me had come to me, when I was still sleeping around, and talked to me just like I talk to people now, I believe that conversation would have started me to thinking about getting my life together.

I often hear teachers say that when they teach a child something new and they see that idea click in the mind of that child, it is one of the greatest feelings of joy and fulfillment that anyone could ever have. Likewise, I cannot put into words the sense of fulfillment and satisfaction I feel when I am talking to people on the streets and I discover that they get the point of what I am saying; and thus, they now realize there is hope for them and there is a way out. However, now it is up to them to accept it.

God has commissioned me to build a faith-based rehabilitation center and affordable housing in San Francisco to help these people rebuild their lives, and I will do this. I have started a ministry called "Red Light District Street Ministry." God has told me to start preaching on street corners in red-light districts. I will soon have a web site where people can read more about God's power to deliver them and share their own testimonies and ideas. I am completely sold out for God; I am ready, willing and able to do whatever He wants me to do and go wherever He sends me.

CHAPTER 18

The Hand of God Upon My Life
The Gene Russell Story

My sister and I were born in a little mining town in Arizona. I was born in November of 1941. My parents went to a Baptist church, and I remember my first awareness of God from a very young age. One day I was in the back seat of our car, a little more than three years old. On seeing the pastor, I kept telling my mother, "That's Jesus, that's Jesus." They had talked about Jesus in the Sunday school, and in my little three-year old mind there was awareness that here was a man who was godly, and I knew that the Spirit of God was in him. It's interesting that I have had little children do the same thing towards me. I think little children can recognize the Spirit of God and be very aware of His dealings early in life. How important it is that we set the right kind of examples, so children see Christ in us, instead of our own nature or something worse.

My mother was spiritually born again when she was 18, only a year before my sister was born and a couple of years before I was born. My father attended the church, but never made a profession of faith. He had gone through a difficult childhood. My grandfather was a murderer and a drunk, a gambler, and a wife beater. I know that my father wanted the things that church represented, but he had that demonic curse that comes down from father to son when someone in the family opens the door for the devil to come in. I was told by a pastor after he had died, because I hadn't seen my father for the last 12 years of his life, that he had confessed Christ on his death bed. We'll find out in heaven whether that was true. I knew that was probably the only way he would come in because he turned away from God when I was 12 years old. I saw the terrible consequences of what happened when my father turned away, and that's what made me want to go in the opposite direction and to embrace the Lord. I was born again in 1953, at the age of 12.

What drove my father away from God were the lusts of the flesh. My father bought a house, and he had all that he wanted really before him, in terms of a good family life. We lived in a good community, but when a certain school teacher moved in across the street who was young and more beautiful than my mother, the lusts of the flesh came out in him and he turned away from the Lord. In fact, in that small town there were such powerful revivals in those years of the early 1950's that I can remember seeing hardened sinners going forward in church, weeping because they were convicted of their sins. Lives were dramatically changed, but I can also remember sitting in the church pews with my father, feeling the resistance in him. It's almost as if you could hear the enemy talking to him, and he was listening.

I was dealt with very powerfully as we sat in those revivals from when I was 8 years old, until I finally gave my heart to the Lord when I was 12. I was very keenly aware, even by the time I was 10 years old, that if I didn't accept Jesus, and if I died at that young age, I would go to hell. I knew that I was accountable for myself and that I was a sinner. I had heard and clearly understood the gospel by that age, and I knew I was responsible for what I had heard. But I never lived a stable Christian life in my youth. Looking back I know why that is, and I can honestly say God has shown me such incredible mercy. A part of that, I believe, is because God shows great mercy to those who have much to overcome.

There was such demonic oppression in our family that as a child I was having horrible nightmares. I didn't know that it was demons, but because of that demonic oppression, I had a difficult time walking a straight walk. I didn't comprehend the ferociousness of the battle. When a person in the family, and the head of the family in particular, opens the door to Satan, he allows demonic oppression upon the whole of the family. When my father committed adultery with the woman next door and threw my mother out — he became very abusive and tried to kill her on a couple of occasions — we had to flee and go to California. It ruined my mother's life; it ruined my sister's life, and neither of them have ever been church members since.

One of those painful things of my life is to see my mother and sister alienated from God. My mother married another non-believer, and although he has been very kind and good to her, he is still a non-believer. She has never been back in fellowship, yet she loved the Lord when she was young. When her family was still together she served God in the church, and she made sure that we were there every Sunday without fail. Then to see her fall away and for over forty years not to darken a church door has been one of the most painful things that I can express. When you know the Lord and you want to fellowship with your own family members, yet they have turned so adamantly away that they will curse you if you mention the Name of the Lord and tell you to keep your religious stuff to yourself, oh how painful that is.

My sister was married and divorced three times by the time she was 22 years old. She had been pregnant every time. Only one of those children lived; the others were miscarried. Because she had witnessed such brutality by my father toward my mother, she was so fouled up inside in terms of what love means. She had so much hatred and bitterness in her heart towards my father because she came home from school and saw my mother begging for her life with my father holding a shotgun at her face and threatening to kill her. It just unwired my sister. She hated men on one hand, yet she craved love. She wanted love and acceptance. Although she said that she gave her heart to the Lord the same day I did, it was not a solid commitment.

My father was married 10 times in life. I don't know how many times my sister has been married. I know of at least six, which is a testimony to the fact that she knows nothing about what real love means. When I phoned to inform her that our father had died, she cursed my father violently, cursed me and hung up. My sister was gifted. She could have been a scientist, a mathematician, or a doctor. She had that kind of intelligence, but her emotions ruined her life. When you don't have the Lord, you don't know how to love and relate to people in a proper fashion, so there is always manipulation going on. That was why the relationship between my sister and mother has also been difficult.

My sister is currently married to a man who is worth millions. I think my sister has improved her lot in life, at least financially, by all the men she has married, divorced and taken money from. Yet she is one of the most unhappy women you could ever meet, because first, a father and a head of a family did not follow after God. He opened the door for the devil to come in, and when the devil gets in he doesn't leave without a fight. He must be driven out by the power of God, and unless there is a willing heart that wants to embrace the things of God, you remain a captive. I believe that God will honor the Word that I and my whole household will be saved, and my relatives will come in. Acts 16:31 says, "...Believe on the Lord Jesus Christ, and thou shalt be saved, and thy house." But, oh what a tragedy to have no life with God on the earth, but only a fire escape from hell at your last days. God help us.

When I was about 19, God dealt with me again. It was my dream to go to UCLA, which was a famous university. I didn't know what I wanted to be or do, but I wanted the opportunity to go to that particular university, and I got to UCLA. In my first semester I went to a Baptist student conference, and out of the blue, I got a letter from a seminary in Kansas offering me a scholarship to come and study. Someone had contact with that seminary and had said that this young man is called to the ministry. I didn't have the deepest kind of commitment to doing God's work, and I rejected that. I was already being influenced by the world in my university career, and I wrote them a letter saying that I really didn't believe that the church has all the answers anymore. I went on through the university, and I got my Bachelor and Masters Degrees from UCLA.

I was a part of the Inter-Varsity Christian Fellowship, and I enjoyed contact with other Christians. But what I want to suggest is that if a young person sees that God is calling them, that they take the yoke and they trust God fully for all of the consequences of their lives. I say this because while I was able to go on and succeed at the university and finally get a Ph.D. and become an English professor, I had no idea that I was walking deeper into darkness every day. Eventually I fell away from the Lord, and for 10 years I didn't go near a church. All that time was wasted. I didn't understand when I was sucking up all the intellectual rubbish, that the devil was setting me up to destroy my life, to destroy the call of God if he could, and to short-circuit all of God's plans for me.

I became a successful college professor, but I had started smoking dope with the other intellectuals, and I became a marijuana head. In fact, I lost my profession because I dropped out of teaching. I stopped teaching, thinking that I was so good and had such great credentials that I could always get back in. Lo and behold, after two years away from teaching, my career was dead, so I had to suffer for 20 years in manual labor before God would resurrect my teaching career. I had to struggle a great deal in life, but mostly it was because I did not take the call of God seriously enough. As I have said, I think that God has been very merciful to me, partly because of my ignorance and the things in life I had to overcome.

I married after I finished my Master's Degree. I taught for a year at Arizona State University. Then I went to the fifth ranked graduate institution in America to earn my Ph.D. Then I went to Europe and taught in Spain on a prestigious fellowship for a year and then came back to America. But by that time my marriage had fallen apart. I had married a Christian girl because her mother was the best Christian in the church. She was very beautiful, and I was working on the false assumption that a daughter must be like her mother. In my spirit I knew it wasn't right, but I disobeyed my spirit. I was not filled with the Holy Spirit, and I really didn't know what the witness of God meant that fully. God tried to dissuade me, but I felt that once I had made a commitment I had to carry through with it. Well, I had five and a half years of living hell. The very thing I wanted to avoid, having seen divorce in my parents, I reaped. That was also one of the key reasons why I walked away from God, because I was so disappointed and hurt by the destruction of that first marriage.

I walked away from God for 10 years. It is a very painful time in life when you don't recognize how far in the darkness you are and then you keep going. Because I was so oppressed, I was spiritually anxious, and I went into Hinduism. I started looking for what I thought was the light, but when you are that far into the enemy's deception, you don't even know where the light is. So I started going to yogis, practicing yoga and learning how to relax. I wound up bowing down before little black idols in India, breaking all the commandments except murder. It took a miracle of God to bring me out of this.

God let me go to the end of my rope, where I had a personal encounter with Satan one night on a riverbank in Nebraska, after coming back from India. God gave me an ultimatum: though He has never spoken to me in an audible voice, when God wants you to know something, you will get the message very clearly. In my heart that night I knew He was telling me, *"Gene, I have kept you as long as I can. If you take one more step in this direction, I will let you go forever."* I knew that was the end.

Praise God that there were people praying for me, and this is one of my miraculous stories in coming back to God and being filled with the Holy Spirit. When I began to teach at the University of Nebraska after I came back from Spain, I taught the American novel course, and there was a Christian woman in that class who began to pray for me. She would witness to me, and she would come in and say, "Mr. Russell, I don't really think the things you are talking about are from God," because I would talk about all the things of Eastern meditation in class at times. She took my name and told my situation to her ladies' prayer group, and every week for four years they prayed for me while I was in the depths of darkness. I can remember wandering around India as a seeker, going to a darkened hole to meditate, but God wouldn't let me go because those people were praying. I know that the night I had the personal encounter with Satan, there was an intercessor praying for me, or I wouldn't have made it through.

I visited one church where the pastor had been a Baptist minister at one time, but he got filled with the Holy Spirit, so they threw him out. This was in the early 1970's, and he had a very successful church. I can remember how, as a student in my university days, I had laughed at the Pentecostals. One of the young men who was a Pentecostal kept trying to tell me that there was more, and I just said, "Well, I'm happy with what I have."

If you're happy with what you have, maybe you're afraid of the light, or maybe you're flirting with the darkness, and there are a lot of questions you need to answer. Time is short, and we are accountable for everything we do. So I wasn't filled with the Holy Spirit until I was 37 years old.

At this church, at the end of the praise and worship, they had a time of turning around and greeting everybody around them. That lasted maybe two or three minutes, and they turned back and started to sing another charismatic chorus. I felt a hand on my left elbow; I turned around, and there was the lady who had been praying for me for four years. She said, "Why Mr. Russell, did you finally get your head straightened out?" I laughed and said, "Yes. I did." She said, "I'd like you to meet the women who have been praying for you all this time." That's one of the wonderful blessings that people who pray get. One day God will show them the fruit of their prayers. I love those women and will never forget them for what they did, because they probably saved my soul. I went to their prayer meeting the following week and met all five of them. What a wonder; what a wonder. That was the beginning for me of really walking with God.

After being filled with the Holy Spirit and coming back into fellowship, I was so filled with remorse for the wasted time. So filled with remorse for bowing down to false gods and involving myself in everything that God tries to spare us from. I had indulged in astrology, palmistry, idolatry, witchcraft, and every kind of occult thing because I had a spiritual hunger. I wanted to know the truth, but I was so blinded that I couldn't find it. When I came back, I was so filled with remorse for that, and I wanted to walk so closely with God; for the first five years of my return with the Lord, I had a supernatural walk with God. I could hear His voice, and I never doubted Him because I knew what He had done for me. His Word became alive to me, and it just leapt off the pages of the Bible. I wanted to go back to a Bible college to fill my spirit back up with the Word of God. I had the intimacy with God that I had always desired, and I had a faith that I thought could never be broken.

But, wherever God works, the enemy works, and it was at the Bible school I once again fell for the counterfeit. There was a beautiful woman again, and I had fallen in love with her parents first because her parents were my classmates, and they were so godly. It looked like I was going to have the thing I had always desired in life — a godly family and an extended family of godly people. All of her brothers and sisters were really committed Christians. But it wasn't right and you can't make right what God hasn't made right. Again I lacked instant obedience to the Lord, and I tried to insist on my way. If you insist on your way, you are breaking one of the commandments that Paul gave in his epistle to Titus. If you want to be an overseer, one of the first qualifications is that you must not be self-willed. "For a bishop must be blameless, as a steward of God; not self-willed..." (Titus 1:7). Even in one area of your life, if you are self-willed, you can undercut all that God wants to do.

The consequence was that just being in an emotional attachment, opened the door for me to be severely wounded spiritually, because that family situation blew up in my face. Her parents turned on me as did the lady, and I walked away wounded like I had never been in life. I had always been able to instantly forgive, and I had always been resilient, but I never knew that you could have your spirit sliced open and ripped in half. For a couple of years I was so wounded I didn't even want to see people. I virtually became a hermit. I couldn't find work, and I was literally starving. I can remember walking the streets looking for scraps from the garbage cans. I went to the school because children would throw away their sandwiches or their fruit, and I would find it and eat it. So I went through some very bitter, hard times. I think God allowed me to suffer, so that I would never lose compassion for those who are down and out. I would really understand what it means to be homeless, what it means to be out of work and not be able to find work. The good news is that God doesn't leave you there when you are seriously seeking Him.

Step by step, year by year, God brought me back into a place of stability, even though I went through enormous amounts of rejection, because by this time I was a middle-aged man who had nothing. Do you think that most women who are young and are looking for a mate are going to look for an older man who has nothing? — A man who looks weird because he has a Ph.D. but he can't even earn a living? Yet God finally brought a woman who saw something beyond the natural. This was after being single, after my first divorce, for 23 years. God brought to me a woman who could see the good hand of God upon my life. She saw the call and believed in me. We met because we were both doing volunteer work at a Vietnamese Baptist Church. She had a call to missions, and I've always had one because I started doing missions work to Mexico when I was in college; and in fact, after we were married, the first missions trip we took was to Mexico for a week.

I married Gail in 1994, and during the first seven years of our lives together, God took us in missions work through five countries of the world. He re-established my teaching career, because overseas they recognized the value of all the education I had. So I could teach in Indonesia, China, and Taiwan. When I came to New Zealand I could at least teach English as a second language to Chinese students. Now I'm approaching retirement age, but I still have all the building skills that God has given me through the years, so I know that God is not through with me.

I think that if anyone reads this or hears this testimony and is young and wants success in life, then if you want God's blessing in life, there is only one way. It is the Bible way. It is building on a solid foundation. Paul said that he laid the foundation of Christ Jesus. 1 Corinthians 3:10-11 says, "According to the grace of God which is given unto me, as a wise masterbuilder, I have laid the foundation, and another buildeth thereon. But let every man take heed how he buildeth thereupon. For other foundation can no man lay than that is laid, which is Jesus Christ." You have to lay that foundation in your life, and everything you build on it must be built consistently, carefully and steadily. When that happens you won't see instant success, and instant success can be one of the greatest curses, but if you persevere in doing things God's way, the consequences at the end of your life will be great. You're going to have riches and treasures that you cannot possibly even anticipate.

I know that because I have made an effort, with the fact of the missions work that we have done — even though I have never been in a pulpit ministry since I was filled with the Holy Spirit some 27 years ago — I know that I have been back on track with God. God has blessed me enormously just by letting me speak His truth to people in different parts of the world. I will take those riches any day.

If this testimony helps someone, that's the purpose of it. Young people have to follow God's way, and there are no shortcuts. If you have to suffer, take it like a good soldier because promotion will come if you persevere. God is going to reward you greatly if you make a commitment to Jesus and never turn to one side or another, regardless of the cost.

CHAPTER 19

The City Of Bells
The Terry Wilson Story

This is my story of how I found the Lord — or rather I should maybe say, how the Lord found me. It was April, 1965. I had not long turned 17 and had never been in trouble with the law, aside from riding on trains without a valid ticket. I still don't know why my friend and I did what we did that April night. There was no need for it at all. We both had good well-paying jobs. I was working at a cable-making factory, and my friend had a good job with the railways. So why on earth did we go out joy riding in other people's cars?

Of course we were caught by the police some hours later, following an accident where I collided with a horse and cart. (The horse was not injured, by the way). My friend was only 16 at the time, so he was placed under juvenile care. And me being 17, I was bound for the high jump of the big house — H.M. Prison in Pentridge, Australia! So there I was, in the cells of the old 'Moonee-Ponds' Police Station, charged with a number of car thefts and larceny. I remember that I had to wait in that police cell for about two days before I was to appear in the magistrate's court to receive the recompense for my crimes. This was my first experience in a police station cell, and it would certainly not be my last!

As the police officer opened the cell door, I shuddered with both shock and surprise over what my astonished eyes beheld: no bed, but just a bare wooden floor with a pile of dirty-gray blankets and a concrete toilet bowl in the corner of the cell. I gathered up a pile of blankets that were heaped in the corner of the cell and made myself a bed to lie on. My thighs and hips soon became very sore from lying on the hard wooden floor. I slept through those two days. I suppose the shock of it all put me to sleep.

I can remember senior police checking on me throughout the night, or was it day? I did not know. I was wakened for my meals that I quickly devoured, then returned to the merciful escape of sleep. Throughout my experience of prison life around Australia, I was always amazed at the number of prisoners who possessed this uncanny ability to just simply 'will themselves to sleep.' Some men would literally sleep their way through an entire prison sentence. The guy would just close his eyes, and that was it. I soon understood why so many prisoners would refer to their prison sentence as a 'sleep;' it was incredible to see such a thing!

I appeared in court with uncombed hair and my clothing was not looking the best after sleeping in them for two days. I looked a real mess. I soon learned that this is the typical state of a defendant's appearance if he/she has spent the night in the police cells. My appearance in the magistrate's court the next morning was like a dream — or I should say a nightmare. I received eighteen months imprisonment! (It was later reduced to six months on appeal.) The magistrate placed me on a fourteen-day pre-sentence report where I would spend the next fourteen days behind the murky, bluestone walls of Pentridge Prison.

The prison van arrived later that afternoon to deliver me to my place of residence for the next two weeks. I was 'escorted' to the van in the vice grip of the driver. He held me tightly at the back of my pants. He had such a hold on me that my feet did not touch the ground. He carried me to the van with my legs flailing in mid-air! (This was a trip that I grew to be so very familiar with.) He bundled me into the rear of a van that reeked with vomit and disinfectant. I sat on a cold metal bench that was so slippery that I would slide all over the place each time the driver threw the van around a corner. It was a noisy ride to prison with the whining of the differential and the grinding of the gearbox each time the driver crunched through the gears. During each trip, the occupants would eagerly await the day when either the differential or the gearbox would blow up! The gearbox actually did blow out one day in the middle of peak-hour traffic. The occupants were ever so overjoyed. A couple of small air vents were located at the front of the van, and when they were open, we could see where we were going. If not… well, it was all a matter of guesswork. A hard turn to the right, followed by a long loud blast of the horn, brought home to us the harsh reality that we were approaching the 'pearly gates.' There was something about that horn blast that froze my blood, as we turned towards the ominous specter of Pentridge Gaol.

The gates opened like the jaws of some unimaginable monster about to devour its prey. An icy sweat grabbed at my heart like the talons of some infernal creature that was about to tear me apart. Nervous cheers rose up from the others followed by proclamations such as: "Here we are; home sweet home!" or, "The big-house!" A symphony of haunting sounds, indigenous to the world behind those bluestone walls, began to invade my consciousness like a school of starving piranha. Cooking smells assaulted my nostrils that reminded me of kill-day in a slaughterhouse.

It seemed as though I had penetrated a dimensional rift that stood between this world and some alien world which one would only experience in a horror story. The sound of rattling chains echoed in my ears. Another gate squeaked open, which beckoned the van deeper inside the bowels of this vile realm of the damned! The van lurched violently forward for a short distance. Then all fell silent. This was the big moment. We had entered the 'Metropolitan Gaol.' Abaddon waited to greet us!

Remanded and sentenced prisoners were together in the reception area. The "Met" (Metropolitan Gaol) is made up of two divisions: 'D-division' (or the yards) and 'F-division' (for those serving terms of three months or less). D-division was composed of a series of holding yards partitioned by eighteen foot bluestone walls. My first night in a prison cell was a haunting experience indeed: the sound of other prisoners shouting to each other from within their cell; the sound of the prison radio that was piped to the cells via a speaker situated above the cell door; the persistent jangle of keys as the screws (prison officers) walked along the tiers all night long. Most of the chatter was the 'Pentridge telephone system' in action. The prisoner would place a blanket over his toilet bowl to use as a type of suction-like pump. When I heard that 'whoop whoop' sound in my toilet, and the water suddenly disappeared with a loud gurgle, I knew that someone was making a phone call. That radio would drive me absolutely silly each night until it was turned off at eleven o'clock. There was no way of turning it off or lowering the volume, because the speaker was located behind a ventilator grill. Oh, how I wanted to rip that speaker out of the wall!

Through my cell window I could hear the sounds of freedom: the traffic outside; trains rattling along as they carried people to their homes or wherever they were going; people coming home from work or going to work on the late shift. These were freedom sounds you never think of otherwise. Even the smell of freedom would come through the cell window. I could smell freedom!

I would think of things which I would never have thought of before, such as the simple act of walking to the shop, or thinking about how we would spend the next day, or just thinking about going to the fridge to get a little snack. Many a night, I have awakened to go into the kitchen to get a bite from the fridge, to only walk smack into the hard cell wall! The simple act of just deciding to stay home and watch television seemed like a priceless treasure to me at the time.

All these little things that we don't usually think about become so very treasured within the mind of a man laying alone in a prison cell. I hated Saturday nights most of all. Near the south wall of the prison was the Coburg Town Hall. Every Saturday night there was a local dance known as the 'Coburg Swinger.' Prisoners in this part of the Gaol would lie quietly on their beds listening to the sounds of the dance-goers enjoying themselves. An occasional despairing shout could be heard coming from one of the prisoners who was being torn apart by the sounds of freedom coming through his cell window. I was wrenched from sleep by the shrill clanging of a bell somewhere deep in the bowels of the building. Oh, the sound of those bells would dominate my life for so many years to come! The bell controlled my very existence within this hellhole: when to go to bed, when to go to sleep, when to wake up, when to eat, and every other aspect during my time in the Met. Every prison uses a bell to run the life of its prisoners!

My ears were greeted with the shout of orders echoing throughout the division by the screws, and the crash of cell doors flinging open. A loud metallic clatter struck at my door and it flung open. "Out of it... where the hell do you think you are!" roared the raspy voice of a burly prison officer standing in the doorway. I quickly got out of bed and got myself dressed. I quickly ran out onto the steel landing and down the steel staircase to join with a line of other young prisoners who stood in line in the passageway. We were counted by another screw, then the order was given to right turn and quick march. We were led into one of several yards that reminded me of cattle pens.

Many would suffer the hellish boredom of those holding yards — a place where one would vegetate for weeks or months on end — waiting for their case to be heard if not bailed. Each yard widened out in a triangular shape from its beginning at an iron grill gate to end with a covered section at the end. There was a shower and toilet at the far end of the yard, which was wide open for all to see.

The reason for the intrusion of one's personal privacy was that the screw in the tower, where all the yards dovetailed into one area, could watch us at all times. Most of us in the yards did not wear prison clothes, but wore whatever clothes we were arrested in. For exercise, we would pace up and down the length of the yard like expectant fathers in an old movie. I remember when I first saw prisoners doing this constant pacing up and down (known as the 'institutional two-step'). I wondered what on earth they were doing. Before very long, I was doing it, too. I could either sit down all day... or... 'go for a walk!'

Sometimes prisoners would walk up and down two or three abreast. Or even more! It was not unusual to see screws on duty in the prison exercise yards of Pentridge Prison, pace up and down chatting away together. When I first entered the holding yards, I thought that this would be just until after breakfast, then we would do some work or something for the remainder of the day. Oh boy, was I wrong! These yards, like cattle pens, were designed to hold prisoners by their designated category and classification.

Cigarettes were like gold in the yards. I saw men selling their bread roll that came with each meal, for a couple of cigarettes. I saw others selling their dessert that came with the last meal at three o'clock in the afternoon, for a couple of cigarettes. I saw other prisoners selling items of clothing for cigarettes. Cigarettes and chocolate were the currency of the prison. There was some money getting about, but that was contraband. Any sentenced prisoner who was caught buying and selling was charged with trafficking, and suffered a loss of remission or a spell in H-division (the prison within a prison — more on that later.) However, if a non-sentenced prisoner was caught trafficking, he could not be charged under prison regulations, but he would spend time cooling off his heals in one way or another.

Those long hours between four o'clock in the afternoon, and seven-thirty the next morning were indeed long and lonely hours... and without a smoke it was maddening! The prison did not make an issue of remanded prisoners with tobacco because they were still able to get them brought in. If the prisoner had no one on the outside to send him in smokes, money or clothing, he was in real trouble. Back in those days, a remanded prisoner was far worse off than one who was sentenced. From seven-thirty in the morning until three-thirty in the afternoon, we froze, fried, or sat under a meager tin roof in the pouring rain.

I spent many a lazy hour listening to the endless rhetoric of prisoners recounting their exploits in crime and analyzing where they went wrong, and how the police had gotten onto them. There was nothing else to do in that yard but to listen to the stories that were told by prisoners regarding their criminal exploits. I was fascinated.

I was back before the magistrate following two weeks of monotonous interviews and examinations. Being that it was my first conviction, I was given the chance to amend my ways. Four days after being released on a two-year probation, there was a knock at my door. Upon opening the door, I was greeted by my grinning partner in crime. He had also been released on a two-year probation by the juvenile court about a week before me.

And what was the topic of our conversation? Yes — you guessed right. *What did we do wrong that got us caught?!* We decided to do it again, but not get *caught* this time. We stole a car from a railway station car park and made up a set of false license plates. What a mistake that was! Neither of us knew about the sequence of license plates which corresponded with the year that the car was registered, nor did we know of the prefixes of interstate plates, which corresponded with the state in which that car was registered. We made the plates from a breakfast cereal box and cut the numbers from white paper, then glued the numbers to the cardboard that we had painted and put them on the car.

For some unknown reason, the police did not detect us as we drove around town all day in this stolen car. I dropped my partner-in-crime off at home, then began to head to a quiet place near home to dump the car. As I was driving home it began to rain. A police car passed going the other way. I checked the rear-view mirror... their break lights came on and the police car turned around to come after me. Apparently, the license plates were beginning to fall to pieces in the rain, and the passing police noticed it. Then they noticed the odd prefix of the license plate. I was dead!

I was back in the police cells, and back in court again! I was sentenced to three weeks imprisonment. The magistrate told me that I needed a 'short sharp' taste of prison to wake me up! On top of that, I was now facing the breach of a two-year probation after only serving four days of it! There I was again: six days after being released on a two-year probation — back on the 'Disneyland-Express,' and back to the boy's yard. Three days after being in the boy's yard, my name was among several that were called over the loudspeakers to come to the gate at the front of the yard. Those others whose names had been called, told me that we were on the list to Pentridge Prison. A prison officer came and opened the iron-grilled gate to let us out of the yard. About twenty of us were led like sheep out of the holding yards and herded from the Met to Pentridge Prison... to "the City of Bells!"

As we were being marched to the prison, I glanced over my shoulder to see the gaping jaws of those 'pearly gates' waiting to devour more souls. As we continued to move away from the Met and towards the prison, I could clearly see the sights of freedom ahead of me over those haunting prison walls. Our procession of the damned passed through a large, arched iron gate that led us through the industrial section of the prison and on to our final destination. I heard the 'clip-clop' of wooden shuttles weaving the yarn in their looms as we passed by the prison woolen mill. The sound brought back memories of my school days when I was training to be a weaver. (The woolen mill became a place where I would labor many times in future years.) As we passed the woolen mills on our right, I looked to my left to see an open caged yard that was scantily covered with a tin shelter. I noticed some pretty ancient looking machinery therein. This was the 'mat-yard' where coconut mats are made for use in government buildings.

We continued on through another arched gateway that partitioned the industrial section of the prison from what is called the 'square.' A long guard tower sat perched above this second arched gateway. A large bell loomed ominously like some infernal gargoyle from within the tower as if it were ready to pounce upon and devour any that may pass by. Its hellish toll tore deep into the hearts of the people who lived outside of those dark walls. It was the heartbeat of the prison! Nothing happened within the bowels of the prison until that infernal bell shrieked out its demonic commands! Each individual division of the prison had its own infernal bell that dominated the lives of those whom it held captive.

As I looked ahead, I could see the main gate, and that clock tower above it. That clock seemed to leer at us and mock us every minute of every day reminding us of time! To the right, I saw a strange walled section of the prison that I later learned was C-division or 'Dodge City' ("candlelight alley"). But more on that later. Our small legion of the damned made a sharp left turn towards the clothing store where we waited outside until we were called to change into our prison clothing.

I took off my street clothes and was handed my prison uniform that consisted of a gray jacket, white striped shirt, blue denim-type pants, thick gray woolen socks, and a pair of heavy leather shoes. Once we were all changed into our prison clothing, we were called by name into different groups in accordance to the designated divisions where we were allocated. I was to go to J-division otherwise known as the 'YOGS' (Young Offenders Gaol).

We were marched across the square and down a narrow alley that ran between E-division and Dodge City to another high wall with another arched iron-grilled gate. Above that gate, too, was an observation tower that ran the length of the wall. An armed screw in the tower pulled a lever, which allowed our escorting screw to open the large gate to let us through. We followed a path which led us to A-division where the YOGS was a wing of A-division reserved for young offenders. This was my first taste of prison life — the first taste of many prison sentences to come in my life of crime.

All of the prison officers in the YOGS were loud and aggressive... the classical drill sergeant type, but that was not of a significant concern to me at the time. There was indeed a code of conduct to be adhered to among the prisoners in the YOGS. For instance, there was the 'lender.' When a prisoner first comes to Pentridge from the Met, he usually has no cigarettes. He had to fill out what is called a 'canteen slip' where he can purchase items from his prison earnings. This was usually each Thursday in the YOGS. A lender would usually lend a newcomer a couple of ounces of tobacco until canteen day, but it was different in the YOGS; you had to pay back double of what you borrowed from the lender, or no lend!

Most YOGS were put to work in the prison farm. It was not hard work though. As long as you got along with your work, you were left alone. There were not enough cells in the YOGS to accommodate everyone, so a large part of those in the YOGS would be accommodated in C-division over night. Life in the YOGS for a first-timer was not easy at all, and there were many of us. I am led to believe that C-division was part of the original 'stockade' that made up Pentridge Prison back in the late 1700's. I am also led to believe that Ned Kelly resided in one of its 'suites.'

How could I possibly begin to describe C-division, or candlelight alley? Whoever thought up the name 'Dodge City' certainly had a brilliant sense of humor. Only a prisoner could come up with such a name! I was 17, and this was my first prison sentence. It was the year 1965 and I was about to enter into the twilight zone of prison life! C-division was not the place where I was to serve out my three-week sentence for car theft, but it was where I was to sleep, owing to the overcrowded conditions in the Young Offenders Gaol. We were marched to a set of arched wooden gates where our escorting screw gave them a kick. There was a rattle and the gates flung open. An uncontrollable urge overtook me to either shudder in horror or to laugh my head off as I beheld the vision before my eyes!

I beheld two rows of two-tiered buildings where cell doors opened directly onto an exercise yard. The upper tier had a wooden safety rail that led to a wooden staircase at either end of the building. Someone behind me said: "Welcome to Dodge City." I later learned that the term 'candlelight alley' originated some years ago when prisoners were issued a candle to take to their cell each night because there was no electricity. The cells were about nine feet long and five feet wide, with no bed or toilet. A striped horse hair mattress lay rolled up on the wooden floor, with five woolen blankets neatly folded on top of the mattress with an old pillow on top. No sheets were issued with the bedding.

Our toilet consisted of a wooden type of commode stool that held a steel bucket. A three-liter plastic bottle held the water supply for the night. If you had a bowel problem, well... what a night you were in for! A set of earphones hung from a plug in the wall, which was our radio that was piped through from the radio cell in B-division. A single 60-watt light bulb illuminated the little cell until it was switched off from the outside at 9:30 p.m. The bell would ring each morning, and the doors would be opened. Each prisoner would collect his toilet bucket and make his way to a large open sewer situated at the end of the yard where he would empty its contents into the sewer. Oh, those poor fellows who lived in the cells either side of that sewer!

It was quite common on a wet morning to see a prisoner slip on the wooden steps while carrying his bucket to the sewer. The poor man's feet would slide out from under him and his arms would fling into the air cascading the contents of his bucket all over the place! I would hate to be nearby when this happened. Dodge City was not only a sleepover for the young offenders; it was also a division that accommodated a large number of homosexuals. Each afternoon, we were brought up to Dodge City from the YOGS to fill our water bottle and ready ourselves for lock-up at five o'clock.

The Salvation Army placed the Gideon's Bible in each cell of the general prison population. Most Bibles were the old King James Version. Prisoners often used the rice paper of the Bible to roll their tobacco in. I was not ignorant of the Bible, because I did attend a Methodist Sunday school in England on rare occasions. Plus, I received top honors in Bible Education while in secondary school. My Sunday school teacher was also my teacher at the public school I attended. I was trapped! So with nothing else to do, I opened the Bible and began to browse through its rice paper pages. Certain parts of the Bible began to get my attention, and I wanted to investigate the parts that had caught my attention.

I decided to seek the guidance of the chaplain of one of the large denominations whom I believed would help me along the way. What a mistake that was! I met with the chaplain in his large luxurious office, and began to ask him questions that had arisen in my mind during my Bible reading. He appeared to be more interested in his image with the prison administration and what his public image was as some kind of savior to the prisoners. His attitude towards me was that I was incapable of perceiving the teachings of the Bible, and that it was only reserved for the clergy to know such things. He looked at me as if I was some sort of a bug that needed to be stepped on. I returned to my cell and threw the Bible in the trash thinking no more about it!

The prisoner loses all perception of the outside world and sees the world within the four prison walls as the *real* world. The other side of the wall becomes an illusion — a non-reality — a fantasy world. Each time that I was released from prison, I was cast into a world that was totally alien to me. It was a world that I could not relate to in any form. My physical body was no longer in prison, but prison was in me! The man was out of the prison, but the prison was still in the man. This is something that only an ex-prisoner could understand.

At home, I would wake up early each morning thinking to myself that I would snooze until the first bell (the wakeup bell), then I would get out of bed. It would be late afternoon by the time that I realized that I was not in a cell but in my own room at home. Not only that, I found it very uncomfortable to be in a room that did not have bars on the window, or to open a door and step out into the street. I was so accustomed to having a prison officer open just about every door for me.

Oh, and another thing: This may sound really odd to someone who has not spent some time in prison away from the opposite gender — all women's voices would sound the same. It would take at least a week or two to begin to discern the different voices. I was expected to come out of prison and straight into a job to earn a living for myself. Remember: Mentally, I was still a prisoner. My mode of thinking was that of a prisoner. My reactions to situations were that of a prisoner. I was not able to perform in the workforce as a regular member of society. I did not last long at all. I had lost the ability to properly function in the outside world.

Each time I had completed a sentence, the prison staff would often refer to my release as 'my annual leave.' Holding down a job was something I could not do because I was so accustomed to the slow pace of work in prison workshops. I suppose I could ramble on through another fifty pages concerning my life in and out of prison over the years, but if I did, I would be losing sight of the purpose of this article. I am not writing a testimony to my shame, but to the glory of God who freed me from my shame, and gave me a whole new life.

Prison is an existence where one has the firsthand opportunity to experience the nature of the heart without the falsehoods that hide its deceiving nature. I was serving time in the punishment section of Pentridge Prison known as H-division. H-division, also known as "hell division" – "the slot" – "the go-slow" – "the punch factory" - or - "the labor yards."

H-division is more or less a prison within a prison that was set aside for those who breach prison regulations. I was placed in H-division for escaping from a prison farm: one of three such escapes. I lay there in cell 23 after suffering the humiliation of the usual strip search that we were subjected to each afternoon before being put in our cell until the following day. I could hear the chirping of the birds outside of my window, and the sound of traffic on the road that ran alongside the prison wall. My mind was in preparation for the long hours ahead in the cell... three-thirty in the afternoon until six-thirty the next morning.

Someone spoke to me, yet I was the only one in the cell. A voice spoke again. This was not a voice in the regular sense. The voice seemed to come from inside of me, yet also around me. I was bordering on blind panic! The voice spoke my name, but the odd thing was somewhere deep in me, I knew that voice. I wanted to leap off my bed and pound on the cell door demanding to be taken to the prison psychiatric division. I became convinced that I had gone stir crazy and finally blown a fuse. I quickly envisioned the next ten or so years of my life spent in and out of mental hospitals!

"Terry, you know who I am," came the voice again as I began to feel the uncontrollable urge to start pounding on the cell door. "No, you are not going mad. I am here," said the voice again. The voice continued: "You know who I am — don't you, Terry?" In utter astonishment I answered: "You're Jesus!" I could not stop the words from coming out of my mouth! "I am He," came the response.

Feeling a little easier now... but still seriously questioning my sanity... I listened as the gentle, but powerful voice spoke again: "Look at your life. It is up to you to change its direction. You can either continue in the way you are going, which will end in death, or you may follow Me. I have a job for you... the choice is yours!" "I will follow you," came my response, still holding serious doubts regarding my sanity.

Jesus told me that I was stained with sin and He needed to come and live in me. He told me that He couldn't live in a dirty house. It had to be cleansed from the stain of sin in my heart and life! At that time, I had no comprehension of the message of the gospel, or the need to confess my sin to Jesus and to invite Him into my heart to make me a new creation in Him. "Therefore if any man be in Christ, he is a new creature: old things are passed away; behold, all things are become new." (2 Corinthians 5:17).

Even though I attended a Methodist Sunday school as a child, I was only taught how to memorize Bible verses. Those Bible verses came rushing back into my mind during the coming days. I realized the facts: that I had to repent from my sin, both original and personal; that I had to be made clean through the blood of Jesus that was shed for me on the Cross; that I had to be born again! Jesus Himself helped me through the 'sinner's prayer' so that I could be made a new creation in Him! I invited Jesus Christ the Lord to come and live in my heart, and to become the Lord and Savior of my life.

Even though I still held reservations about my sanity, Jesus impressed upon me that He would prove that this is really happening by making me like Daniel in the lion's den during my stay in H-division. However, Jesus did say that in times to come, I would try as hard as I could to get away from Him. I strongly protested at this by telling Him that I would never do that. Jesus also made known to me on that day in cell 23 that I would be confronted with a wall of criticism and unbelief regarding my testimony. Jesus impressed upon me that in days to come, I would experience the cold religious hand of rejection because of my testimony — from none else but the professing church itself! This confused me because I believed that those in the church (the religious institutional system) would welcome what I had to share. This was proven to be so true a short time later when I tried to tell the prison chaplain about what had happened to me. I was indeed confronted by a wall of outright unbelief!

One morning as I was breaking rocks in my little 'labor yard,' a big burley prison officer came in yelling and making a big noise. He had full intentions of beating me with the baton that he held in his hand. These random beatings of prisoners were commonplace in H-division at the time. He raised his baton, and began his downward lunge. As he was in the process, I saw a large hand manifest, taking hold of the prison officer's baton arm. The prison officer's face turned a sickly pale color. He ran out of the yard like a frightened mouse! He never came near me again.

Late one afternoon, not long after lock-up, prison officers began to systematically go from cell to cell beating the occupant with their batons. I became very afraid. Again, a voice spoke to me. I knew it to be the voice of a personage who belonged to God. "Fear not; the Lord is with you!" exclaimed the voice of 'someone' near the cell door. The occupant of each cell before mine was beaten. They came to the cell next door and beat up the occupant; they passed me by and continued on to the cell next to me!

Bibles were not available in this part of the prison. The only Bible (as it was called) was a copy of the rules and regulations of H-division, which every prisoner had to know by heart. However, there was a small bookshelf in the corridor that contained a few books. We had to reach out and grab one if we were quick enough. On more than one occasion I grabbed a copy or two of some *Full Gospel Businessman's Fellowship International* literature that helped me a lot in those long hours in cell 23. John 15:26 says: "But when the Comforter is come, whom I will send unto you from the Father, *even* the Spirit of truth, which proceedeth from the Father, he shall testify of me."

The following three months was spent in H-division, but during that time I had the Lord Jesus Christ with me. I got to know Jesus more and more each day. I knew that the Holy Spirit was with me because He would tell me things of Jesus and not of Himself! No further acts of violence were committed against me by the prison officers. In fact, I was treated in a manner that was quite odd indeed! The first day that I was released from H-division and into the general prison population, I made a beeline for the library to get my hands on a Bible. The Word of God confirmed all that was shown to me by the Holy Spirit in cell 23.

It later came to my attention that a prisoner in an American prison came to know Jesus in the same way that I did. He wrote a book about it. *Me* write a book? Never! I was placed in E-division which was a division made up of dormitories instead of single cells. That was fine with me because the dormitories had television, and besides, I could share my experience of Jesus with other prisoners!

I was put to work in the woolen mill again — *where else?* I was able to share my experience of Jesus Christ to many both at work and in the dormitory, and many gave their life to Jesus. I was released from Pentridge Prison in June of 1973. I made a beeline home to my wife and a son who was born while I was in prison. I caught my wife by surprise because I was released a few days earlier than was expected.

However, the life that I thought we were going to live as believers in Christ Jesus was not to be. A lot of pain was yet to come. My wife was a member of a major church denomination, and attended church every Sunday with her family. I was considered as somewhat of a heathen at the time. I sat my wife down on the couch and began to share my testimony with her of Christ Jesus in the hope that she would receive Jesus into her heart and life as I did. I immediately discerned that she was not understanding what I was sharing with her. She simply told me that I was suffering from some sort of a delusion owing to my long period of solitude. It soon became apparent to me that my wife could not deal with this 'new Terry' — the new spiritual creation God had made me. She became convinced that I was suffering from some type of a psychotic break, and I needed to receive some sort of professional counseling.

I began to show her from the Bible what God expected of Christian believers in comparison to what her church doctrine taught. This was a thing that she refused to accept. Eventually, at the urging of her family, the marriage fell apart and we separated. That was in October of 1973. I then recalled an incident that happened in Pentridge while alone in my cell just before my release, as I lay in my cell thinking of the life ahead with my wife and son. I felt the Spirit of the Lord say to me that this marriage would end four months after my release because this woman was not the one chosen by God for me. I had married this woman for all the wrong motives. Hence I was released in June... separated in October!

At this point, I really began to believe that I was suffering from a type of psychotic episode, and that indeed what I experienced in cell 23 was a dangerous delusion. Satan's lying spirits worked overtime to try to deceive me. As my marriage was falling apart, I tried to seek out Christian counsel, or to find believers such as myself. All I could find were those who claimed to be Christian, but the Spirit of the Lord was not in them as I saw it. I found no help or support anywhere, so I threw in the towel and gave up. My wife divorced me in 1976, and I never saw her or my son again, who is now in his 30's. I was branded as a dangerous religious nutcase. It was not too long before I found myself back on the old merry-go-round of in and out of prison, not caring if I was alive or dead... free or in prison. My reality was within the four walls of a prison, and the outside was a world of illusion.

In 1982 I met a woman by the name of Joanne, whom I had known for some years during a return trip to Melbourne, Australia. She was a friend of my family. Joanne, like myself, had experienced a failed marriage that lasted no more than eighteen months. The last thing on either of our minds was marriage. However, things clicked between us and we were married that same year. It was during October of 1986, following Joanne's onslaught of questions about the Bible, that I repented from my sin and backsliding. Joanne had no idea about my going astray, or of even being a Christian. Not until I shared my testimony with her did she come to know Jesus as her Lord and Savior. Those early years were simple years. Joanne and I enjoyed the pure uncomplicated outpouring of God's unconditional love in our lives. Things were simple in our day-to-day walk with Jesus.

We became friends with a young professional church-going couple (whom we shall call 'Mr. and Mrs. Church'), believing that it would be nice to have Christian neighbors. We lived in the house opposite of this couple in our quiet Darwin suburb. We attended the same church that was no more than three or four kilometers away. We did not own a car, so we traveled by either bus or bicycle. Child seats were fitted to our bikes so we could carry our two youngest boys with us. It soon became clear to us that Mr. and Mrs. Church did not want to offer us a ride to church each Sunday, so we decided to bike it with our children. Of course, the ride to church was an uphill trip in thirty-plus (Celsius) degree heat, but the ride home was much better!

Joanne eagerly looked forward to meeting other Christian women in whom she could share her new-found faith. She began to attend the women's midweek Bible studies, and would come home discouraged instead of encouraged. When I asked her what was wrong, she would tearfully tell me that the women at the study would ignore, or rebuke her for not finding a Scripture verse fast enough. Not one of the women took into account that Joanne was totally unfamiliar with the Bible!

We began to notice that people in the church would never accept our invitation to come over for lunch or coffee. Or could we not help but notice that many in the church would regularly visit Mr. and Mrs. Church, but yet not even give us the slightest greeting. This troubled us greatly. It was clear that we were being discriminated against because I was unemployed at the time. Around this time, our son Patrick was diagnosed with a delayed mental developmental condition, along with a degree of autism. These 'church people' told Joanne and I that Patrick's condition was the result of hidden sin in our lives, or that he was full of demons. Such an attitude clearly comes from the Dark Ages. The 'church people' were blind to the obvious reality that Patrick was one of those babies who had an adverse reaction to the child immunization program (MMR). Through fervent prayer, God dealt with our son's condition and began to open up his mind and ears. He soon began to speak and converse with those around him. Over the years, God continued in delivering him from the murky depths of his condition. In fact, he is now working at a full-time job!

There seems to be this misconstrued belief among a lot of Christians that if a person does not work they should not eat. "For even when we were with you, this we commanded you, that if any would not work, neither should he eat." (2 Thessalonians 3:10). This Scripture deals with something other than what was being leveled at us. It is referring to the custom when one is invited to stay as a guest in someone's home. It was customary for the guest to do some work around the house of the host in payment for their food and keep. In no way has this to do with anyone who is unemployed; but for some obscure reason, this erroneous belief is locked into the minds of many church people.

We have heard it all: "Poverty is a curse" and all that goes with it. We could write volumes on this subject, but this is not the time or the place. On the night in question, I was having my usual time with the Lord in prayer when a very unusual thing happened. Hearing cries for help, I stopped praying and ran outside to see who was in trouble. *There could have been a car accident, and people hurt,* I thought to myself. All was quiet. There was nobody about. I went back inside to continue with my time with the Lord. Again, I heard people crying out for help, so again I went outside. There was nothing. Again, I heard the cries for help! This time I said: "Yes Lord, here I am. I am ready."

Immediately, a veil was lifted from my eyes and I beheld a vast pit that was full of people. I could not count the number of tormented people who were looking up at me. I stood there in absolute shock! The people within this vast pit were aware that I could see them in their torment. Their cries for help seemed to be an endless chorus of pain! *What is going on here?!* I exclaimed to myself and to God. The Lord impressed Luke 16:19-31 upon my heart when Jesus spoke of Lazarus and the rich man. He made it clear to me that what He referred to in Luke 16:19-31 was an actual event and not a parable, otherwise the Word of God would have declared it to be a parable!

The great ocean of tormented people before me were those in Hades. Those who were waiting to be cast into the lake of fire on the Day of the Lord! Revelation 20:11-15 says, "And I saw a great white throne, and him that sat on it, from whose face the earth and the heaven fled away; and there was found no place for them. And I saw the dead, small and great, stand before God; and the books were opened: and another book was opened, which is *the book* of life: and the dead were judged out of those things which were written in the books, according to their works. And the sea gave up the dead which were in it; and death and hell delivered up the dead which were in them: and they were judged every man according to their works. And death and hell were cast into the lake of fire. This is the second death. And whosoever was not found written in the book of life was cast into the lake of fire."

This part of Hades was shown to me because the people in this pit whom I was looking at were those who in life believed that they were right with God and they believed to hold the truth. They believed that they had their own way to God and did not want to be told anything different! They had chosen not to believe the simple message of the Cross, but elected to follow popular humanistic concepts that offered them compromise and not the need to repent from their sin!

I continued to gaze into the pit of tormented souls. My eyes transfixed upon these souls experiencing the foretaste of hell. I wanted to reach into this pit and pull them out, but the Holy Spirit moved upon me and told me that there is nothing that can be done for these people because they had chosen to reject God's only provision for their salvation in Jesus Christ the Lord during their earth lifetime. Their cries were great, and I was deeply disturbed by what I saw. Even today in 2005, as I write this, I am still affected by what I saw in that pit. It drives me to go on sounding the warning to those in the church not to take the work that Jesus did for our salvation on the Cross for granted. And not to treat the message of the Cross as foolishness, as many religious people do through their idolatry! "For the preaching of the cross is to them that perish foolishness; but unto us which are saved it is the power of God." (1 Corinthians 1:18).

The Lord allowed me to behold the pit of Hades to tell people of what I witnessed. Those within the pit are condemned to hell! Those still living in the flesh still have the hope of repentance in Jesus Christ, and getting it right with God through the Cross of Jesus. If we enter the grave without Jesus, only Judgment awaits us, and we await that Judgment in the pit of Hades! This is why I was allowed to see and hear what I saw and heard... to warn those who are deceived into thinking that they have their *own* way to God!

Kind permission was given by Precious Testimonies to share this testimony.

CHAPTER 20

Delivered from Hurt of Abuse and Scars of Sin
The Shelia Holcomb Story

When I was born, my mother was only fifteen years old. Now years later, and after I went through the process of forgiving her and working through many things, I am now able to look at her life through her eyes to try to better understand how she must have felt. Someone gave me this advice when I was really struggling with all of this. I was told that *maybe I could forgive easier if I tried to see her life through her eyes and not the eyes of a hurt child.* Do you know what? It worked! I can understand her more clearly now. She was not mature enough to take care of herself, much less a baby.

Mother would send me here and there to whomever would be willing to take me at that particular time. Most of the time it was my grandmother. Several times throughout my life she would decide that she wanted me back, and she would come and uproot me again. I never really knew any stability in my life, and I always felt as if no one really loved me or wanted me.

Then at the age of nine, she came and got me and took me away from my grandmother. At this point of my life, Grandma was the only mother I had ever known and I was very attached to her. Anyway, my mother came and took me to Illinois where she lived. By this time she had remarried, and she had two more children by her new husband. He hated me, and the only reason I could figure out why, was simply because I was not his child. Now this was not my fault, although I did blame myself for many years.

He started just physically abusing me, but at the age of nine that changed when he raped me. This abuse went on until I was thirteen, and I finally told my mother. She didn't believe me; actually no one believed me. Finally I just let it drop and I buried all of those feelings of anger and hate for years. That has now all been dealt with and forgiven, and now it is all under the precious blood of Jesus, praise God.

I told my mother that I wanted to go back to Memphis to live with my grandmother. She consented just because she felt I was causing so much trouble, and she did not want to be bothered. My grandmother was now also remarried, and I resented her new husband for taking her away from me, too. You must remember I was only a child and I felt like she was all I had, and now I had lost her, too. I was very hateful to her husband and caused so many problems. He was very kind and loving to me, but I just could not accept what he was offering to me.

My grandmother, finally after a long struggle, went to the courts and told the judge that I was out of control and they just could not handle me any longer; so they removed me and placed me in a foster home. The home I went to was wonderful, but at that time I could not see things clearly. All I could see was that the only person who should love me had now turned her back on me as well. I just wanted my grandmother, so I ran away. The courts then really called my bluff, so as a ward of the state of Tennessee, I was placed in a Catholic all girls reform school for three and a half years. Now as I look back, I can honestly say it was one of the best things that ever happened to me. But at that time all I could see was that I was totally alone, unloved, and unwanted in this great big world.

Now I will jump ahead some. In 1987 I lost my three children to their father and I totally lost it. I turned heavily to alcohol and eventually that turned into crack and cocaine. By this time I had lost everything including my dignity, as I had turned to prostitution to support my drug habit. I was arrested several times on various charges, but I was never convicted and I never served any time. I know that God was taking care of me even back then in my sin; He saw what I would be one day in Him.

I give GOD all the PRAISE, HONOR AND GLORY for all that I am today and all that I will be. The drugs and my roaming had taken me to many places, but on December 20, 1990 I came across a man who told me about Jesus and how He could deliver me and make my life an example to others. I had not eaten in a couple of days and he asked me if I was hungry; so he took me to a restaurant and bought me something to eat. The entire time he shared about Jesus Christ with me. He told me Christ could and would set me free if I was willing. He told me how He (Jesus) would give me a new life without all the pain and turmoil I was living in.

Of course, being a Christian does not eliminate us from pain, trials and tribulation, but with Christ in our hearts He will give us the strength to overcome and withstand even in the worst times. I began sharing my life story with this man and he still said Jesus is the answer. Boy, was he right. Right there I gave my heart to the Lord, and I decided to live for Him and serve Him for the rest of my life.

I had been singing for many years and I had destroyed my voice through drug abuse. I just abused the gifts that God had given me. So I prayed and told the Lord that if He would heal and restore my voice, I would use this gift for His glory for the rest of my life. Now God has done exceedingly and abundantly above all that I could ask or think. The songs that I sing and others that I have written, they are all His, and I am only an instrument holding the pen. It does not matter where you are, Christ will come to you and meet you, if you are willing to let your life go and let Him be God *of* and *in* your life.

I have had so many miracles in my Christian life as I am a walking miracle myself. One of these miracles really stands out to me and I would like to share this with you as well. About four or five years ago I was diagnosed with an incurable bowel condition. The doctors were not real sure what it was exactly, but they had come to the conclusion that with ulcers all through my body and many in my bowel system, they said they wanted to do surgery and remove some of the bowel. My reply was that I wanted to get prayer for this, and that I believed that God was going to heal me and I would not need the surgery at all.

They went ahead and scheduled me for another scope the following week, just a few days after Christmas. Then on Christmas Eve, I placed a long distance call to a minister friend of mine and asked him to pray for me. He said no problem, but he would need to call me back in a few minutes. While waiting for him to call back I got about ten Bibles and placed them open on the floor in a circle, with one opened in the middle of the circle. When he called me back I knelt on the Bible in the middle and said, "Pray." When he prayed for me, the fire of God hit me and went through me; I had such a peace come over me.

I went over to my bed and fell asleep. In Scripture, Adam was put into a deep sleep in Genesis when God removed the rib to create woman. God did the same for me as I lay there sleeping; He performed surgery on me to heal my body. I slept for seventeen hours, and when I awoke the bleeding had stopped and so had the pain. I knew without a doubt that I was healed by the precious hand of the Master. I was on about $400.00 worth of medicine a month and I went into the kitchen and threw it all in the trash. I did go back for the scope when I was scheduled, and the doctors were amazed there were no ulcers anywhere. I just praised God for His healing power!

I am now an ordained minister and I am married to a wonderful man who is also a minister. We know God has put us together for a ministry and we are enjoying serving the Lord together. I also am now a Southern gospel singer/songwriter. The Lord has blessed me and I will continue on this road He has placed me on, for my desire is only to serve Him. I will travel anywhere I am invited to give my testimony or to sing or both. God is wonderful and it is to His glory that I am writing this. If one soul is reached in any way, then this is worth everything. Again I cannot stress enough that this is for the glory of God that I am here and that my life is what it is today, for without Christ we are nothing, but through Him we are joint heirs with Him.

He is our Deliverer, Savior, Helper and Healer, and any problem we may have is never too great for Him to help us. We just have to take it to Him and leave it at His feet and in His care. I thank God, for His power is still healing, still saving, and still delivering. He is good all the time. I have made my mistakes but His grace is sufficient. God loves us and if we truly repent and confess our sins, He is faithful and just to forgive us and cleanse us from all unrighteousness.

If we can help anyone out there, please contact us at the information provided below and we will do our best to help in any way we can. If you have questions about loved ones who may be on drugs or other addictions we will try to answer your questions. If we do not know, we will do our best to find the answer for you. If you have loved ones that you need prayer for, we will gladly join you in agreeing for that person for the Kingdom.

Please, always remember we are all human and we will all make mistakes, but just confess to God those mistakes and get them under the blood of Jesus as soon as possible. God still loves us and He will help us in all of our situations.

God bless and keep you all. I give full permission to anyone who can use this testimony to copy it and give it out or to share it publicly, but please, give all the glory and praise to God. Thank you.

Also, please feel free to email us at rainbow@imws.net or visit our website at Rainbow Ministries of Texas. We would love to hear from you!

CHAPTER 21

Delivered From Dark Feelings and Vultures
The Andrea Do Santos Story

I started learning about the occult when I was 12 years old. Those first 12 years were filled with a lot of pain. My parents had an off and on again relationship, sometimes spending months apart, then getting back together. When they *were* together my father was physically and emotionally abusive to my mother, my brother and me. Mother was not very strong emotionally and suffered from a mental illness, and because of this, I felt she was never there for me.

To add to the instability in my life, I was sexually abused by a son of some friends of a family. This started when I was 8 years old and continued until I was about 12. To add to my insecurities, I started at a high school where I didn't know a person. I was teased and picked on a lot by the other kids and this only made matters worse.

I became very angry at my parents, the world, and especially God. I used to watch a lot of horror movies and read books about ghosts and spirits. It terrified me but fascinated me at the same time. The time came when I decided to look into witchcraft and Satanism. I believe my anger toward God was my motivation for doing so. I felt that it was His fault my life was so horrible, and by doing the *opposite* of what He stood for, I would be better off. I was so deceived and so blinded by my anger and hate.

I was probably fortunate the Internet didn't exist, because the demonic information I had access to was limited to a few old books from the library. I think it is a lot more dangerous these days for a child to search out the occult, because the Internet has so much information I never had access to. The books I read taught how to call on spirits (demons really, in my ignorance of course) by their name and offer yourself to them in exchange for power. I did as they said and sure enough it was not long before I started having weird, supernatural events occurring. These would happen at night time; it would terrify me. I would feel the presence of entities in my bedroom, and they would torment me. Eventually, I decided not to play with the occult anymore because of it. God gave me enough grace to realize I was delving into something I really did not understand, and it was better to turn back to God. What I didn't realize was a door had been opened in my life to the demonic, spiritual realm — in my mind — and a willingness to close that door was not the same thing as running away from it.

My coming back to God was blurred as well. I did not really understand truths of sin and repentance. I was raised Catholic, and the necessary spiritual rebirth that Jesus speaks of in John 3 had never been taught to me. Instead, I believed God was always taking care of me and life would go on as normal. I was no longer reading about witchcraft or practicing demonology so I thought everything was okay. Was I ever wrong!

A few months after I had stopped practicing these things, I started having suicidal thoughts. I also kept having recurring nightmares that made me terrified to sleep. My parents were too busy in their destructive relationship to notice what was going on with me. It came as a total shock to them one night when I overdosed on my mother's sleeping pills. I was 12 years old.

What I have learned since becoming a Christian is that the devil is set on trying to destroy humans, especially those who have any tenderness towards God. I believe he does this because he is jealous of the love God has for us. His main weapon or strategy is deception. He fills the world with lies in order to entrap us. He sets up cheap imitations of what God offers us in order to entice us into his world. As an angry and neglected 12-year old, I felt powerless about all the things that had happened to me; therefore the devil was able to see my rebellion and vindictive attitude and deceive me into believing I could obtain power if I made alliances with his demons. The reality was that those powers entered my life and started using their weapons against me, such as confusion, despair, and lies like I would be better off dead, and that my parents didn't love me.

If I had turned to God instead of Satan when I was 12, I would have had God's power to protect me and offer me hope in my childhood. I would have been comforted by the love of God rather than destroyed by the hatred of the devil.

Regressing some... the hold of the occult over my family began long before I was 12. We come from Uruguay, South America, which is a country that officially has Catholicism as its religion but where the practice of black magic and belief in the spirit realm is common. It was not unusual in my family to believe in superstition alongside with God, or to seek healing from sources other than Jesus Christ.

My maternal grandmother in particular was constantly looking to psychics and spiritual healers instead of Jesus for reassurance. This might seem weird to Westerners but is very common in many Third World countries. People are not as educated and ignorance is prevalent. People are very superstitious and fearful. I remember being told that if I read the Bible too much I would go crazy. This sort of thinking encourages further ignorance and takes people away from their potential they have in God through a relationship with Jesus Christ.

Thus my grandmother, in her desperation for hope, looked into the wrong sources. The consequence of those actions meant the seed of the occult had been planted in my family, ready for the devil to harvest.

My grandmother has suffered for her actions. She has experienced severe mental illness throughout her life. Again, if we look at what some of the devil's tools are, we find he uses confusion and despair against us; and this is exactly what one suffers when mental illness is at its worse. I believe that by opening herself up to forces outside of God, she has suffered from the demonic attack of mental illness; and although blinded to it, she has brought a curse not only upon herself, but to her offspring. There are consequences for our actions. The consequences of our actions almost always gets passed onto our offspring. I saw this in my family with my mother suffering from mental illness as well. Because of her illness, this became a block in her relationship with me. My father was violent and had addiction issues that were passed onto me, and I had a vulnerability to addictions and abusive relationships.

At age 14 I was experimenting with alcohol and other drugs, and sex. I continued to have recurring nightmares to the point that I avoided sleeping. I also had started self-mutilation as a way of coping with all the negative emotions I felt inside. During that time, my parents had split up again. I started living with my mother and brother. My mother had a severe nervous breakdown and my brother and I ended up homeless. I went to live with my boyfriend's family and my brother went to my father's house.

Inside me was a very angry and cold heart. I felt no sympathy for my mother — just hatred. I felt abandoned by everyone. If there had been a little grain of faith left in me at that time, it was not there for long that I'm aware of. I stopped believing in God or anything good. I didn't believe in the devil either, but that didn't stop him from still having a grip on my life.

At age 16 my friends and I began playing with Ouija boards. We contacted the supposed spirits of the dead (again, demons — without our realizing it). This seemed like a fun thing to do, but it wasn't long after this that I started waking up feeling like someone was choking me. There would be a female presence in my bedroom at these times. Whether this was a nightmare or for real I was never sure, but for years I would wake up terrified — either because I was being choked, or because of the female entity hovering over me. Eventually I came to realize this had been brought on my playing with the Ouija board, and so I stopped playing with it.

I was full of despair inside. Over the next few years I was homeless often, sleeping on the lounge room floor of a friend's home. During that time I managed to push my way though my final year of high school.

There was a lot of chaos in my life. Most days I had to search for a reason to live. Depression, anxiety and suicidal thoughts were part of my everyday life. The nights were the worst. My mind would be full of tormenting, negative thoughts. I felt extreme loneliness, being totally on my own. My family had been torn apart, and my friends — though they were there for me in their own way — could never fully understand what was going on inside me.

Other people saw the outside of my life, that I was a good student and very intelligent and talented in different areas. Yet because of this, they could not comprehend the conflict inside me. They believed I had everything to succeed in life and as such had nothing to get depressed about. Yet when you are so full of despair, confusion, anger, self-pity and self-hatred, also when you have a demon sitting on your shoulder telling you how worthless you are and that the only way to escape your pain is through death, it doesn't matter how talented you are. It is next to impossible to see beyond your inner turmoil.

At age 19 I began attending a university. I was addicted to a variety of drugs and living a very promiscuous lifestyle. My behavior was erratic and eventually I had a nervous breakdown. I was diagnosed as having a bipolar disorder and spent nearly a month in the psychiatric ward.

During my time of psychosis I had an experience with Jesus. He showed me all the things in my life I had looked into: drugs, the occult, relationships with men, and how I had put my faith in each one of these things and gotten rotten results. He then asked me: *"Why put your faith in all these things when you can put your faith in Me?"*

This experience stayed with me, and as soon as I was able to leave the psychiatric ward I started to read the Bible. The more I read, the more I was amazed. I had so much respect and admiration for Jesus. I could relate to all the things I was reading, but I was still not healed spiritually or emotionally. I was yet very vulnerable and it was not long before the drugs, promiscuity and mental illness came back into my life full-swing.

I had certain rules I placed on myself in order to keep my addiction to drugs in line. These rules kept me within a certain limit. One rule was like making sure I never had direct access to a drug dealer. That way I always had to go through someone else, and my addiction was limited by my access to the drugs. A rule was never borrowing money to buy drugs.

One night things got totally out of control. I had people I didn't even know coming over to shoot up drugs in my home. I had been selling my possessions in order to get more drugs. Then I broke one of my rules. I rang my mother and lied to her about needing money for something, when really I wanted money to get another fix. That was my lowest point. I was so full of shame and self-hatred that I could no longer look at myself in the mirror. I counted out all my pills (medication for my bi-polar condition), and wrote a suicide note. I was ready to die, but then the phone rang. It was God.

God was on the phone in the form of my friend Matthew, who had recently become a Christian. He said he felt it heavy on his heart to call me even though it was quite late at night. He asked me if I was all right, and when I explained to him what I was about to do, he praised God that he had called me.

Just then there was a knock on my door. It was the guy I used drugs with plus an ex-boyfriend of mine (one who had been particularly abusive). They wanted to score some more drugs.

I stood in my lounge room with a very keen awareness of what was going on. In my bedroom there were the pills and suicide note: Option 1 - death. At the door there was the devil and drug addiction, plus abusive relationships and chaos: Option 2 - slower death. On the phone there was God who loved me so much that even when I was about to kill myself He managed to send someone to stop me: Option 3 - Rescue and Life. Which way was I going to go?

I chose God. After that night my life started to change. My friend Matthew started taking me to church and for about a year I started learning about Jesus and had Christian fellowship. My mind is very foggy about that time of my life. I was on medication for the bi-polar condition; and being in another abusive relationship, I was very depressed. But I know my faith in God was cemented. Before, I had stopped believing in Him. Now, as I recovered from drug addiction and struggled to survive with an abusive partner, I reached out to the Lord and He was there for me. When no one else was there, God was there.

The only problem was that I did not agree with many of the things the church was teaching. I did not realize it then, but now I see the devil was driving a wedge between me and Christianity as part of his counter-attack. He did not want to lose me to Jesus and so he started whispering in my ear things that were not true, and I believed his lies.

I also had some well-meaning Christians testifying to me. What they didn't realize was that their method was overbearing. For someone who was struggling to find their own feet and identify in Jesus, it was too much to have someone constantly on my back about the Lord. If anything, these people pushed me away from my faith rather than encouraged me in my spiritual growth. I wish I would have had the strength of character back then to politely ask them to back off, but I didn't.

In one year God took me out of the drug addiction, chaos and mental illness my life had come under, but the devil was also putting up a good fight, and I walked away from church. I believed I was doing the right thing (and in some ways I was), but I did not seek out another congregation. Instead, I decided that Christianity was one of *many* ways to God, and that I wanted to find out 'What God is' rather than 'WHO is God.' It is one of the devil's craftiest schemes to get a child of God sidetracked.

The seeds of the occult planted by my grandmother now took firm roots, and the thorns and weeds of the devil started to choke the young plant of Christ in my life (Luke 8:1-8 refers). The curse was certainly being passed onto the next generation. (Of course, all blame cannot be placed on my grandmother. We each will be held accountable to God for our *own* decisions and actions — not those of others that affected us).

I met a male who was interested in paganism (goddess-based religions), mythology and other areas outside of Christianity. I was enamored by this man and for the next four years hung on his every word. He was never able to offer me more than friendship (and looking back his friendship was very destructive), but I was blind to all this at the time. From being around him I started to study paganism and other religions. I believed in a goddess who was multi-faceted, and I started to practice rituals in honor of the goddess and the elements. Without realizing it, I was back under the control and domain of the devil, yet in the early days it *seemed* I had discovered something beautiful and ancient. The goddess was older than the Christian God, and many of the attitudes of Christianity appeared to be traced back to pagan mythology. I came to believe that Christianity was just a newer version of paganism, with the character disguised in different forms. This is how deceived I became.

In this time I learned about the psychic realm and started working as a psychic. I did tarot readings, read auras and worked with spirit guides. I also taught psychic development to others. I also read many self-help books and received a lot of counseling to come to terms with all the things that happened to me growing up. Without realizing it, seven years had passed from when I had my first nervous breakdown. (Let me say here that even though the counseling and therapy helped a lot, it was not until I was born again in Christ and filled with the Holy Spirit, that I truly began experiencing peace, joy, love and other fruits of the Spirit).

As a psychic, I believed I was helping others. My readings were more spiritual than anything else. I advised people in their own spiritual development as well as predicting future events. I prided myself on the accuracy of my readings and in my role as a spiritual advisor to others. I had a deep, vast knowledge of the world's religions, and was able to mix and match my beliefs to create an overall understanding of life, or so it seemed. I came to believe in reincarnation, and that "ultimately there was no wrong or right because every experience in life was a lesson from which we could learn and grow." I believed every soul was constantly learning and so it didn't really matter what you did, because every experience was valid as an opportunity for learning; and as an entity that was constantly evolving, we all had to go through a variety of experiences in order to achieve enlightenment. I believed life was an on-going process, and what we did not learn in this life we would have ample opportunity to cover in following lives. Though there are particles of truth woven in and out of these beliefs, I was totally deceived to the truth in the Bible about deception.

I believed Jesus was a teacher and I lived my life according to His teachings (i.e., love your God/goddess above all things and your neighbor as yourself), but I did *not* believe in the virgin birth of Jesus Christ or that He rose from the dead. Obviously I didn't believe He was fully God either.

The Bible clearly warns of people like I *was*. For instance, take a look at 1 Timothy 4:1-2: "Now the Spirit speaketh expressly, that in the latter times some shall depart from the faith, giving heed to seducing spirits, and doctrines of devils; speaking lies in hypocrisy; having their conscience seared with a hot iron."

On top of all this, I believed I was especially gifted as a psychic, and that this gift was inherited from my mother and grandmother, who were both touch healers. I believed mental illness was really just a spiritual gift — one that had to be monitored closely — but a gift none the less (Yeah! A "gift" all right — from the devil!); for this gift enabled me to experience the spiritual realm in a way others could not.

I believed my role as a spiritually gifted person was to pass on my knowledge to others and help them in their spiritual development. Meanwhile, without me even realizing it, my life was in chaos! The majority of people in my life were drug users, and they slowly started to take over my house. My own addictions had come back into the foreground. I was doing less and less psychic work and more and more drugs. My rational thinking went down the toilet as I concentrated more and more on psychic messages to determine the outcome of my life, rather than make clear-headed decisions about where my life was heading.

The devil had me wrapped around his little finger! By playing up to my ego, and my need for approval, he had fed me the lie of "helping others develop spiritually" via my psychic work, while all the while leading me into a maze of confusion and chaos. If I was so spiritually advanced, why was my life such as mess? And who was I to guide anyone else?

By convincing me that life was a series of lessons, and that there was no right or wrong, I was able to justify my outrageous (and destructive) behavior as part of my own inner spiritual growth process, while never really acknowledging how pointless this process was "ever learning, and never able to come to the knowledge of the truth." (2 Timothy 3:7).

I had not really learned from my past mistakes. Here I was seven years from my first breakdown, and I was addicted to drugs once again. I had people using my home as a party house; I was sexually promiscuous, practicing in the occult and suffering from depression/suicidal thoughts/anxiety. Within, I was dead, empty and broken.

Yet, I was blind to all this. The devil played up to my pride, and my own pride made me blind to all my faults. I was defensive about my life, constantly claiming everything was fine and in control, when in reality my life was a mess. I hid behind my status as a spiritual being and pointed my finger at all the people around me as the ones with a problem.

2 Timothy 3:1-5 reads: "This know also, that in the last days perilous times shall come. For men shall be lovers of their own selves, covetous, boasters, proud, blasphemers, disobedient to parents, unthankful, unholy, Without natural affection, truce-breakers, false accusers, incontinent, fierce, despisers of those that are good, Traitors, heady, high-minded, lovers of pleasures more than lovers of God; Having a form of godliness, but denying the power thereof: from such *turn away*."

God began to break through my spiritual blindness when I became pregnant with my son. I met my son's father under strange circumstances and my instincts told me to stay clear of this man. Yet a number of tarot readings, interpreted dreams and "coincidences" all pointed to him as my soul mate. Rather than listen to my head, I listened to these phenomena and we were intimate. A few weeks later I found out he was married. A week after that I found out I was pregnant. It was then that I began to see how deceived I had been by all the psychic stuff.

During the pregnancy, as I watched all my "friends" slowly drop away or turn against me, I started to reach out to the Lord. Once again I had no one else, but God was there with me. I still did not have a totally clear understanding of the spiritual and emotional crippling effects the occult, mental illness and drug addiction had launched against me, but I was starting to realize I had gone off track. I asked the Lord for strength, guidance, an easy birth and a healthy baby. He answered my prayers. As much as each day was difficult, Jesus was with me every day of my pregnancy, and I could feel His presence making me strong and calm, keeping me positive and encouraged.

After my son was born, I continued to pray. One night I found myself saying, "Thank you, Jesus, for dying for my sins and rising again." I was shocked at myself! I realized I believed in the risen Christ! I didn't understand how or when, but I now believed!

From that point on, God began to pave the way for me to come back to Christ. I know I am the prodigal daughter who has come back to the Father, after squandering my life in the world (Luke 15:11-24 refers). I can now look back on my life and see where I went wrong, and I know it is only by the grace of God that I survived my time in darkness.

My heart's desire is to now be used of God to help others who do not know Jesus, especially those who are slaves to addiction, and/or have been deceived by the devil through their involvement in the occult. I am so grateful for what I have in Jesus: not only have my sins been forgiven and I have eternal life, but I am being filled with joy, peace, love and patience; and slowly, I am learning self-control.

The first thing God asked me to do when I came back to Him, was get rid of all my books except the Bible. (My books were mostly occult, New Age and self-help based). I could relate to the Bible when it says in Acts 19:19: "Many of them also which used curious arts brought their books together, and burned them before all *men*: and they counted the price of them, and found *it* fifty thousand *pieces* of silver." (The total value of the scrolls would be about $364,000 of today's American dollars!). It was difficult to give up my books and all the things related to my work as a psychic, but I understood that what Jesus offers us is greater than anything I could find in those books. Really, we only need *one* book to guide us in this life, and that book is the Bible. (1 Timothy 4:7: "But refuse profane and old wives' fables, and exercise thyself *rather* unto godliness.")

Since I became born again, Jesus has taken away the negative (un-Christlike) people from my old life and brought me to a beautiful, sincere, loving and supportive Christian church family. He has healed me of all my addictions, including cigarettes, and is healing me of my addiction to over-eating. Food is still an issue for me since I use it to stuff my emotions down. I am also very overweight, but I know God is working through me; and in time, this issue will be another area I can use to testify about Jesus to others.

My purpose for writing this testimony is to help those out there who have not heard the truth, and/or are trapped by the occult. I know when I was with that crowd, the evil had me so deceived that I truly didn't think I was doing anything wrong. The danger in psychic phenomena is that it presents a possible reality outside of God's authority. I now know that anything outside of the Lord Jesus Christ is just a cheap imitation. There is only *one* living God who created all things. God has a plan for every single person on earth. When someone goes to a psychic, they are ignoring God's plans, and instead they are seeking the advice of demonic spirits. By putting our faith in demonology (psychic phenomena) we are opening ourselves up to occult powers, and turning away from the blessings Christ has planned for us. By inviting the occult into our lives we are sowing seeds of destruction for ourselves, loved ones, our children, and even potentially their offspring.

Mental illness, drug addiction and the occult are very much linked. The practice of taking drugs — drugs of course alter our perception — is a form of witchcraft. Indeed many pagan religions use drugs and altered states to connect to the spirit realm. Many people who have mental illness are well aware of the spiritual realm. They experience demons, angels and many other things as part of the confusion of the condition.

The devil convinced me that my illness was a blessing. This lie was aimed at my pride. By looking at my condition as a "gift," I was in denial about the harmful effects it had on my life. The combination of the bi-polar condition along with the psychic realm and goddess-based beliefs (as well as drug use) was catastrophic. The sad thing is that most of the people I came across who worked as psychics, healers, and other New-Agers, are the victims of addictions and mental illnesses. (Depression and anxiety are prevalent). As much as they claim to be helping others, when I looked beneath the surface there was always something else going on like greed, pride, selfishness and competitiveness. The force of denial is so powerful, especially when your ego is being fed with status and glamour. Only the light of Christ can reach those who are so far gone in the dark.

The danger in believing in reincarnation is twofold: First, there is no sobering fear of judgment for our actions before a holy God after this life. The Bible clearly speaks of this judgment in Hebrews 9:27: "And as it is appointed unto men once to die, but after this the judgment:" Second, it encourages people to be completely self-serving. If every experience in life is just a lesson that we need to learn, then we are accountable to no one, including *God*, as the first point addresses. We then rationalize: "What does it matter if we hurt others, betray our families and friends, and indulge our every whim? We can chalk these things up to just another experience to learn from." This is where the deception comes to play, and where the devil plays at our ego. For we are called by God to be more than our whims; we are called to be reflections of His greatest glory — Jesus Christ and His love.

We are called to reach beyond our own selfish desires and strive to reach out to others in love and compassion. We are called to look into our hearts and lives, seek out our faults and bring them to the Lord for forgiveness and repentance. We are given one life on earth to serve God, and it is only through this understanding that we reach true enlightenment, with Jesus as the source of light and truth in our hearts and lives. It is He who allows us to go beyond our human limitations and reach a level of existence greater than anything we could have ever imagined on our own.

I desire to be a servant of the Lord by His grace, as spoken of in 2 Timothy 2:24-26: "And the servant of the Lord must not strive; but be gentle unto all *men*, apt to teach, patient, In meekness instructing those that oppose themselves; if God peradventure will give them repentance to the acknowledging of the truth; and *that* they may recover themselves out of the snare of the devil, who are taken captive by him at his will."

Is the Bible truly the *only* book we really need to know about God — to know how we are to have a right relationship with Him and others?   Here is what 2 Timothy 3:16-17 says: "All scripture *is* given by inspiration of God, and *is* profitable for doctrine, for reproof, for correction, for instruction in righteousness: That the man of God may be perfect, throughly furnished unto all good works."

It was in October 2004 when I finally gave up trying to run my life my own selfish way, and admitted to God that I had made a mess of my life and asked God to take over the reigns. I promised to do only as He wanted me to do.

And so the process began: first of all it was the 12 Steps of Narcotics Anonymous.   Next, it was doing my best to reconcile with my baby's father. That's when I learned that it is *obedience* that matters and not the results. After that it was the Alpha course.   My mother had been praying for at least four years for me to do the Alpha course. Thanks to God, my mother, and the Alpha course... I was born again! I finally accepted Christ as my Lord and Savior and committed myself to Him.

Since then, the Lord has been filtering out all those dark feelings — the anger, the pain, the hurt, the pride. It has been a long labor, but since that day the Holy Spirit entered my heart and I was born again, I have been filled with much peace and joy, and slowly ... ever-increasing compassion and love.

In front of my friends and family, on May 1, 2005, I was baptized in water, to show the world that my life belongs to Christ. I wanted my old life washed away. I wanted to show the Lord how grateful I am for all He has done for me: for keeping me safe in the palm of His hand even when I went exploring the darkness; and for shining the light so that I could find my way home.

I am now willing and honored to commit myself to Christ. In front of everyone I want to say, "Jesus is now my Drug! I am addicted to His Love and God's Grace. Jesus is the relationship I rely on. He is the friend who will never abandon me, the Man who will always be there to listen and comfort me. He is the reason for the joy in my life and the peace in my Heart. He is the knight in shining armor, sent to save me from all my sins, and the darkness and the lies of the devil. He is my Lord and Savior! Knowing that, by putting my faith in Jesus, instead of in the world, I am Saved!"

Since being baptized, my church *(Full Blessings Church; Frankton, Victoria, Australia)*, has asked me to share my testimony with the Youth Group. It seems that all the intelligence and experiences I had wasted in the past, God is finally putting to good use! My church believes I will be helping others come to Jesus, and in my heart, this is all I want — for others to find the beauty of the Kingdom. Slowly my life is starting to come together, and I am excited that even though I can't see where I am going, God is holding my hand and lighting the way.

He'll do the same for *you*, if you'll allow Him to.

What I've discovered in my personal relationship with Jesus Christ is that God is the same from the beginning to the end. He is the One true God, expressed in three persons: God the Father, God the Son (Word), and God the Holy Spirit. He is the righteous judge and the loving Father. When He came to earth as the Son, He was given the Name Jesus and He was the long promised Messiah, the Christ. Jesus Christ showed us how much He loved us, by going to the Cross to shed His innocent blood for our sins. He took the wrath of God upon Himself that sinners deserve, so they could be freed from God's wrath throughout eternity. He lives in born again believers through the Holy Spirit, when we accept Jesus Christ as our Lord and Savior, and purpose to follow His commandments.

If you can relate in any way to my testimony: if you have been deceived by the devil into looking outside of Jesus Christ and the Bible for your faith, then I challenge you now to turn away from your error — your sin and your rebellion — and invite Jesus to come live in your heart. He will show you where you went wrong, forgive you for your sins and show you the right way to live your life. Not only will His love and Spirit guide you in this lifetime, but you will also be welcomed into the eternal Kingdom of God as one of His children — a place where we will be celebrating the glory of God forever. I hope to meet you there.

CHAPTER 22

Not Afraid To Die
The Jim Sepulveda Story

"Jim, if you own anything of value, you'd better make out a will," my doctor told me after severe chest pains sent me to the hospital. Tests revealed an enlarged heart, a damaged main valve, and two main arteries blocked by cholesterol. I would need double bypass surgery and valve replacement. "We give you only a 10 percent chance of making it," the doctor warned. I was terrified. At age 35 I was too young to die.

Six weeks before surgery God intervened in my life. Much against my own personal wishes, God arranged for me to attend a healing meeting. Once there, I was greatly agitated by what was going on, and was going to leave during the service when suddenly the speaker announced: "The Holy Spirit is telling me there's a man here who is scheduled for open-heart surgery. If you will come down now, I believe the Lord's going to heal you." I glanced around as he waited. Surely he didn't mean me. No one came forward. "God has a work for this man," the speaker continued. "Let us pray and see if the Holy Spirit might reveal the man's name to me."

Incredibly, God did reveal my name, and reluctantly, I went forward. After answering a few of his questions, here's what happened: Suddenly my knees buckled and I fell to the platform, wrapped in a warm blanket of peace and love. A red light appeared toward the ceiling, which came down and touched my head. A pure warm heat ran up my left side and stopped in the area of my chest. Then it felt like two little fingers moved things around inside my heart. "Jesus, I love You," were the words that slipped from my mouth without conscious thought. "I know that I know that You've healed me. I love You." Up to this moment, I hadn't been to church in 13 years, sad to say.

Upon returning to my doctor, I told him about my experience in the auditorium. He wasn't impressed. "Jim, if you don't have open-heart surgery, you won't last over six months." We discussed the situation at length, then a clear thought came to mind: *Catheterization. Do it for the glory of God.* I knew that was a procedure when doctors make an incision in one main artery, then feed a catheter into the heart to take pictures and ascertain the exact state of the heart.

"Doc, listen. I don't want that open-heart surgery. I want a catheterization." He argued, but I convinced him. Several days later I was on the operating table. I was awake during the whole catheterization process. Everything seemed to go very well. Then during the last maneuver I suddenly felt like a white-hot poker was stabbing my heart. Agonizing pain ran across my shoulders and down my side. I began to lose consciousness and felt the doctors pounding on my chest. As dark shadows closed around me, I could hear voices from far away, echoing like sound in a tunnel: *We're losing him... losing him... losing him...*

I opened my eyes. I was standing in a field surrounded by acres of green grass. Every blade of it glowed, as if a tiny spotlight lighted them. To my right stretched a dazzling expanse of flowers, with vibrant colors I'd never seen before. I walked over a nearby hill, stopping as a light began to appear near me. The blinding aura was too bright to look at directly. I squinted down toward the ground, then saw a pair of sandals begin to appear at the bottom of the light.

As my eyes moved upward, I glimpsed the hem of a seamless white gown. Higher, I could make out the form of a man's body. Around his head shone an even brighter brilliance, obscuring a direct view of his face. Even though I couldn't see clearly because of the dazzling splendor, I knew immediately the identity of this Man. I was standing in the presence of Jesus Christ.

Jim, I love you. His voice washed over me... indescribably gentle, tender, peaceful. *But it's not your time yet. You must go back, for you have many works for Me to do.*

The brilliance surrounding Him reached out and engulfed me, immersing me in love and peace. I don't know how long I stood transfixed, but finally I turned away and began walking back over the hill. Then a blue mist of light began to come around me like a fog. It turned into a dark shadow, and everything turned black. Opening my eyes, I realized I was back on the operating table covered with a sheet. I didn't know until later that my heart had stopped beating for eight minutes. They had given me up for dead!

Everyone had left the operating room except for the main surgeon and one of his assistants. They were at the back of the room, filling out a report on my death. As I sat up, the sheet slid down my lap. They turned and looked at me with their faces ghost white. "Get the rest of them in here quick!" the surgeon urged his assistant. The doctors performed numerous tests. Early the next morning the surgeon came to my room and announced he was releasing me from the hospital. "Come back this evening at 8:30 to my office. We'll go over all the results of your new tests."

That evening I told my doctor what I'd experienced during the eight minutes I was clinically dead on the operating table. "Jim," he said, "let me show you something you won't believe." He showed me the new pictures of my heart. Rather than being enlarged, it was now normal size. There had previously been 85 percent blockage in two arteries; now there was none. The main valve was functioning normally. My doctor looked at me, tears in his eyes. "Jim, this Jesus you've been talking about has either replaced or repaired your heart."

Shortly afterward God called me into ministry. Since then I've had the opportunity to share my testimony to thousands both here in America and in

Europe. It's been the thrill of my life to see the Lord use me to touch so many lives — to see people turn their lives over to Jesus Christ and see the positive change that follows, as they grow in their personal relationship with Him. Before this all happened, as I faced the good possibility of dying, I was terrified. Now my fear is gone, *as yours can be,* replaced by the joy of knowing someday I will see my Savior again face to face.

Thank you for taking the time to read my testimony and it's my prayer that it helps you come to believe on Jesus Christ as your Lord and Savior. If there's any doubt that Jesus Christ is the One to put one's trust in for eternal salvation, there certainly wouldn't be doubt any longer if you had seen what I had seen during those eight minutes I was dead.

Let us never forget Christ's promise to humanity as recorded in the Bible in John 20:29: "Jesus saith unto him, Thomas, because thou hast seen me, thou hast believed: blessed *are* they that have not seen, and *yet* have believed." Thomas was one of the Lord's disciples at the time of Christ's crucifixion. After Christ's resurrection from the tomb, He returned in bodily form and revealed Himself to His disciples, but NOT Thomas.

The disciples who had seen Jesus were later telling Thomas what they had seen and heard Jesus say, but Thomas was as doubting as you and I might have been. Thomas said, "Except I shall see in his hands the print of the nails, and put my finger into the print of the nails, and thrust my hand into his side, I will not believe." (John 20:25).

Eight days later, Jesus then revealed Himself to Thomas, also. The words Jesus Christ spoke to Thomas still echo across the universe, and through the soul of every person who longs to be right with God, and grow in relationship with Him: "... blessed are they that have not seen, and yet have believed." (John 20:29).

What does Scripture then say is the *benefit?* "... that ye might believe that Jesus is the Christ, the Son of God: and that believing ye might have life through his name." (John 20:31). There's a great difference between mere religious activity... and LIFE in Jesus Christ, isn't there?

Kind permission was given by Precious Testimonies to share this testimony.

CHAPTER 23

Being Gay...
The Roberta Laurila Story

Right from the day of my birth, there was a hint of future problems. When my mother first saw me, she expressed her love for me, then remembered she only had a boy's name chosen. Thus, Robert became Roberta.

During childhood, my mother's heart condition and crippling arthritis kept her from doing the usual things with me that my friend's mothers did. I became a loner and a daydreamer. At the age of eight, I was imitating everything my older brother did, from smoking cigarettes to dating girls.

When I was 10, I "fell in love" for the very first time with my lady school teacher. This crush lasted for three years until our paths separated when I began my freshman year in high school. My heart was grieved until I met a beautiful brunette in my class and new love sprang up in my heart. Of course I couldn't speak of this love to anyone. I began to realize that somehow, I was different. My whole being cried out to love and be loved. Living with my secret longings through those teen years was so difficult.

I tried being like my friends and began dating young men when my father would allow it. When he wouldn't, I became angry and rebellious. I built a bad reputation for myself and as the small town tongues began wagging, I started withdrawing, and became antagonistic toward all.

My Christian mother was very patient during those years, but my father was under conviction for not accepting the Lord. His cursing raged out of control nearly every night as he verbally abused my mother. These times sent me into a rage. It was during this time in my life that I decided no man would ever treat me like that.

I also rejected my father for getting Mom pregnant again. She was in ill health and she hadn't wanted another child. I had also heard many stories of my father's first wife dying at childbirth and that filled me with fears of having children. No way was that for me.

Then at 16, my "steady" boyfriend tried to rape me. That event really confirmed to me that sex was filthy and an abomination.

After high school, all my girlfriends were getting married. I became fearful of being left out. In desperation, I gave in to my brother's suggestion to meet one of his friends, 12 years older than myself. In less than three months, I married this man whom I didn't even love. After two years, I divorced him and began writing to a man in the Armed Forces who had loved me before my marriage. The decision to marry him came when I learned he would soon be going to Germany in active combat. I could receive an allotment check and wouldn't have to live with him. What a farce! Less than two years later, he

126

came home and I soon divorced him.

Not long after, the Holy Spirit began to convict me of my sin. I had attended tent meetings in a Pentecostal church when I was a child, and marched to the front night after night to get saved. But I'd given it all up when I realized I couldn't be good in the days following.

When I began to feel pangs of guilt, this made Satan angry. Soon after, I was introduced to a lesbian who had been in that lifestyle a long time and knew the ropes. She was a bad influence on me and soon I began drinking, which I had never done. The second night, she invited me to spend the night with her. I began meeting other lesbians and partying far too much. Not long after, I was fired from my job.

I soon met a girl who was my "type" and we lived together for eight years. Because of the guilt and drinking, my fits of jealousy and temper became uncontrollable. Then I left my first friend and began living with another. After a year I nearly killed her in the car after drinking too much wine. Needless to say, she left me for good.

I was home alone the afternoon of October 7, 1955. With fear and panic in my heart, I made the decision to take my own life. I was too ashamed to commit myself to an institution to find help for my troubled mind. Pride was still very much alive, even though I thought I was beyond help. I wondered how to call my friend to ask for her forgiveness. I wanted so much to be forgiven, but it seemed out of the question.

I started for the kitchen to turn on the gas jets. I had already had a few drinks to try to give me courage. Just before I entered the kitchen door, I fell to my knees in front a chair. With tears streaming down my face, I cried out, "God forgive me. God forgive me!"

Only later did I realize that I was saved at that moment. The Holy Spirit came to live within me, and began leading me in ways that confirmed my salvation. But in rebellion, I still held onto my old friends. I had two lesbian relationships after my salvation. *God doesn't expect me to quit loving women*, I reasoned. Of course, I couldn't stop without supernatural help. And I didn't have anyone else to help. This was years before God raised up former homosexuals to begin ministries.

After 10 years that I had received Jesus Christ as my Savior, I was still living in sin. God began allowing me to feel the consequences of my rebellion. I could not have survived the trauma that followed without the Lord's care and mercy. God allowed the devil to pour out his wrath in such a devastating way. I still shudder at his trickery. With demonic signs and wonders, Satan convinced me that God wanted me to live with another woman while involved in Christian ministry.

The climax came following the suicidal death of a dear friend whom I had betrayed. It was from that shocking emotional experience that my stubborn will was broken. I promised God that I would not let her death be for nothing.

Then came the vision. While living in what seemed to be a hell on earth with my lover, God came to me one night. I was alone and in deep despair. The Lord gave me a spiritual vision of a worldwide ministry. This outreach would reach homosexuals who wanted a close relationship with Jesus Christ and who wanted to be set free from their sin. As the vision unfolded, I knew God was saying I must leave this lifestyle forever. I was to begin interceding for Him to raise up individuals from the gay lifestyle and others, truly called by Him, to begin specific ministries to homosexuals.

Six years after the vision, God directed me to write my personal testimony of deliverance from lesbianism. My story entitled "Gay Liberation" was published in book form in 1975. It was the first of its kind and not many bookstores would accept it, due to the subject, which was "hush-hush" at the time.

Much has happened since that time. While I continued to intercede, God began calling forth former gays to minister. God has blessed my friendships with many of the "pioneers" in the Exodus movement, such as Frank Worthen, Robbi Kenney, Ed Hurst, and others. I have been blessed also to see many ministries begin on foreign soil. What a wonderful God He is!

God has kept me at a low profile. At times, I have rebelled concerning this. But deep down, I know I was called to intercede for others to be led by the Holy Spirit into the entire world. Even as I write these words, tears are flowing down my cheeks. Surely God will complete His perfect plan to reach the many millions of the lost who have been so rejected and lonely so many years.

I weep for the church, blinded by the enemy so it cannot see the need to teach gays. So many Christians cannot truly believe that God can set these people free. My great desire now is to reach those in the gay church. I am believing God to also work a miracle there.

Our God reigns!

CHAPTER 24

I Went To Heaven
The Judith Webb Story

I was raised in what I'll call a "heathen home." God's name was a byword, and that's all I knew about God. All of that changed on March 18, 1960. I received into my heart the revelation of the gospel, fell in love with God's Son Jesus Christ, and found out that God was real.

In 1964, I was filled with God's precious Holy Spirit, and I literally changed inside and out. After seeking God and being on a 21-day Daniel fast (no pleasant food), I was teaching a woman's seminar on marriage when God chose to reveal some important spiritual truths to me.

We had started each day of the seminar with praise and worship. On one particular morning the Spirit of God came as I was praising Him. As I placed my hands on each side of the pulpit, I was caught up in the Spirit. A very large angel, at least 12 feet tall, came into the sanctuary and picked me up in his arms. As he did so, I became as a little child, perhaps five or six years old. He then carried me to the throne room of God.

The first thing I saw was a throne, glory clouds, and very large arms. I saw Jesus standing there. This was all at one glance. I could see His piercing eyes and they looked straight into my being. I then saw the bright light of approval come into His eyes. I can see those eyes everyday because they have been imprinted in my mind. Spiritual things never grow old. When He gave His approval with a slight nod, the angel approached Him and put me in His arms. He then turned towards the throne and Father God's enormous arms reached out to me. Jesus then placed me into the arms of Father God and I felt myself go into the glory cloud. I remember those arms giving me a warm hug. At the same time, I seemed to be on the outside watching with my mind. When I came out of the glory cloud, I went back into the arms of Jesus, and then back into the arms of the angel. The angel then returned me back to where it began. When I came to myself, I was still holding onto the pulpit, and no one realized that anything had happened.

As I thought back, I realized that in an instant, I had seen the River of Life and the trees that were for the healing of the nations. This scene seemed to go on as far as I could see. What I saw was so beautiful, clear and perfect. Words cannot adequately describe how beautiful heaven really is. I have never forgotten that experience. I don't know what all took place that day, but I thank God for this awesome experience. He knows what we need.

I've served God for many years now, and He's proven to me over and over again how wonderful He truly is. Heaven is filled with such love and peace. My friend, you don't want to miss heaven and what God has prepared for those that love Him. Those in Christ Jesus have such a bright future. If you have not received Jesus as your Lord and Savior, then you need to. He has such a great love for mankind. I strongly urge you to receive Jesus as your Lord and Savior. *He loves you so much!*

CHAPTER 25

Snakes in an Atheist's Grave
(By B.E. Perigo)

Sometimes we read of some blatant atheist who challenges God to strike him dead, or to prove His existence, but it is rarely indeed that God takes up such a challenge in the form in which it is made. However, in the case we are considering, God did accept an atheist's challenge, and accepted it in such a remarkable way that the infidel's grave is preaching effective sermons to many people week after week and year after year. The cause related is not one that occurred in the distant past, and which no one can investigate today. Anyone with an automobile and a little spare time can see for himself. Large numbers of people are doing that very thing. It was my privilege to make the trip to North Benton, Ohio, to see the cemetery of which I speak.

The atheist in question was Mr. Chester Bedell, who died in 1908 at the age of eighty-two. He is said to have been a very bold and blatant skeptic, and was out-spoken in opposition to God and the Bible. I was told that he was a very mean man and that neighbors and others were afraid that if they crossed him they might get up the next morning to find their barn burned to the ground or other damage done. It is declared that he left one dollar each to his two Christian daughters and his 2,500 acres of land to his unbelieving sons. He was in many lawsuits during his life. It is said that he occasionally attended the Presbyterian Church in the town of North Benton, and that his presence threw such coldness over the service as soon as he entered, that it almost broke up the meeting.

The direct challenge which Mr. Bedell hurled at the Almighty was this: "If there is a God or any truth in the Bible, let Him infest my grave with snakes." He wrote a book against the Bible entitled *Universal Mental Liberty*. Sometime before his death he had an imposing statue of himself made of bronze and placed upon a large pedestal. In his uplifted hand is a book with the inscription, "Universal Mental Liberty." Under his foot is a scroll representing the Bible, with the word "Superstition" in large letters. A minister visited one of Mr. Bedell's daughters for information, and she said her father belonged to The Society of Damned Souls and had said that if there was a God, he wanted Him to infest his grave with snakes. His daughter says that when he was dying he said, "Oh, that I had never had that monument built," and wished he were able to go over to that cemetery and tear it down, but it was too late.

And what was the sequel? SNAKES! When the grave was dug the sexton killed two snakes and when the casket was brought to the grave another large snake had to be removed before it could be lowered. That was twenty-four years ago, and since that time the family lot has been full of snake holes around the curbing. The snakes can be seen any day you visit the cemetery, except perhaps the day after a rain. The sexton told me that under the monument and around the grave is a den of snakes. And an equally remarkable fact is that this burial lot is the only place in the cemetery where snakes are ever found — so the sexton declared to me in a talk that I had with him. The North Benton Cemetery has a regularly employed sexton who takes excellent care of the grounds.

The trip which I made to North Benton was by auto from Pittsburgh, Pennsylvania. North Benton is just eighty miles from Pittsburgh. Mr. and Mrs. Miller, who took me in their car, had made two previous trips. On one they counted eight live snakes. On the other they saw sixteen that had been killed and piled up by other parties. As we neared the cemetery I felt nervous and somewhat excited. Yes, there was the monument just as it had been described to me! I counted ten angry looking snake holes around the grave. I have pictures of five snakes, including two large ones crawling from between crevices in the cement curbing. The sexton had killed a black snake six feet six inches long just before we came, and he saw the head of another — the largest he had ever seen — which crawled back before he could kill it. I inquired why there were bloodstains on the statue, and the sexton said boys would come and kill the snakes and throw them up around the neck of Mr. Bedell's statue, then he would have the task of taking them down. That is almost enough to make the old atheist turn over in the grave! As many as twenty snakes have been killed in a day, and the sexton says that the more you kill the more there seem to be. One expression heard in and around North Benton is, "Well, if Bedell did ask for snakes he sure got 'em!"

The sexton informed me that people come from all over the United States to see the statue and grave; and that previous Sunday, 200 or more people were in that cemetery. Mr. Bedell's sons and some people near the cemetery are pretty much stirred up over the publicity that snakes have brought to the place and have been talking of taking the statue down, feeling that the statue and snakes together are a reflection on their cemetery. Some have told the caretaker that they wished that he would tear the monument down, but he replied that he did not think that it should be torn down, as it preached too many sermons.

Kind permission was given to share this testimony by www.churchofgodliterature.org.

CHAPTER 26

I Saw A Heavenly Choir
The Byron Wright Story

In October 1996, I was having heart procedures and tests done at Saint Vincent's hospital in Indianapolis, Indiana. I was already a Christian when I entered the hospital on that day. At the end of one procedure, the surgeon and my family were checking the results when I became very ill. I expressed how ill I was feeling to the surgeon. He said it was caused by the dye that they used in the procedure. Even so, I became sicker and my color changed from gray to white to blue. My son expressed that he thought it might be a heart attack. As the surgeon closely checked me, he determined that I was having a heart attack.

I was immediately taken to surgery, and on the way, I remember looking at the ceiling, and felt myself go through it. I did not feel the ceiling touch my body. I was traveling at such an exceptionally high rate of speed. I felt that I was in a tube-like tunnel. I had never felt such speed in all my life. It was a wonderful feeling, almost similar to an airplane taking off, but it took my breath away. I looked at my feet and saw a small, round light at the end of the tunnel I was in. Within seconds, I came to a bright light and into a large room where a choir of people were singing along with a large orchestra. The music was the most beautiful that I've ever heard in my life. I found myself singing with them. The director then turned around and asked me to join them as I was singing with all my might. As I walked towards them, I felt so comfortable and right at home. There was such wonderful peace; it was like a place one would search for all their lives. I'll never forget this experience. It's embedded in my mind and heart. It's as real to me today as if it was yesterday.

I was so enjoying this fellowship, but then I heard the voice of the surgeon saying that they were losing me. I remember saying to the surgeon that it was alright. It has been alright ever since 1950. He asked me what 1950 was all about. I told him that it was when I received Jesus Christ into my heart as Lord and Savior. He remarked that was good.

The next thing I knew was that I was awakening in my room the next day. Since that time, God has witnessed to me that He had a specific reason for sending me back. He wanted me to be a prayer intercessor for which I've found such joy in doing. From that time to present period, I've experienced many answers to prayers. There have been healings, deliverances from drugs and alcohol, salvations, cleansings, people being set free from habits, job placements, and resolvement of marriage problems. I give all the glory to God. I'm so thankful for having the privilege of being His servant. Jesus is such a wonderful Lord and Savior, and He only wants the best for mankind. His love is so great for all of us.

CHAPTER 27

It's Never Too Late
The Pat Sullivan Story

God truly is a God of miracles. This is a tribute to the awesome power of God who helped me not to take my mother-in-law's rejection personally. Had I not been a Christian, I would have been so overcome by her indifference, and rejection of me, I never would have been able to get out of my selfish little feelings, to love her unconditionally! Because I prayed, I was able to overcome how she had treated me, and care about extending the love of God to her the last months of her life. (By Ceci Sullivan)

Her name was Pat Sullivan... She was an interesting woman and I'm sorry to say, I only knew her the last several weeks of her life. I went to take care of my mother-in-law who had refused to acknowledge I was alive the 14 years I've been married to her son. She had ignored my presents, and had been indifferent to all my phone calls and letters! I only heard of her critical, bitter, and condemning attitude towards me and her son through others. She chose not to end her life with all that vile in her heart towards us, and I'm so thankful that's not how her story ended.

The love of God ended up overcoming the bitter, critical heart she had... LOVE PREVAILED IN THE END! I told her, though she rejected me, I would continue to love and give to her, and have faith that one day things might be different. I knew I didn't want to leave this world not doing everything I could to reach out in love and faith towards others. *Who wants to die with a heart full of bitterness, only caring about how others have treated you!* I asked Jesus to deliver me out of the kingdom of selfishness, to be able to care how I LOVE OTHERS, MORE THAN HOW OTHERS LOVE ME, AND HE DID... AND MIRACLES TAKE PLACE WHEN THE SPIRIT OF GOD'S LOVE PREVAILS!

Her son, Gene, had become a Christian in 1972. Upon this news, she offered him psychiatric counseling. She lived life hard and partied hard, worked hard, and fought hard most of her life. She not only taught my husband to be a champion boxer, and Pipercub pilot, but she was one of the first B-25 female bomber pilots, in WWII.

Gene grew up on an airport, helping his mom with her crop-dusting business. She taught him many valuable lessons, and he is very grateful for all she had done for him. Even though he didn't conform to her wishes in staying to run the airport, he loved her deeply. This brought a breech into their relationship, which only broadened greatly upon him becoming a Christian. Her hard heart towards God, estranged her from him. Instead of hearing from the voice of love and faith, she only had ears to hear from the voice of accusation... the bitter critical thoughts that divide relationships.

After all my many attempts to reach out to her, it was hard for me to not faint in thinking I would never know her. Then one day we received a phone call that his mom had a heart attack in the doctor's office and wasn't expected to live. Well, we had prayed for her continually over the years and my heart sank at the thought of things ending like this!

Gene was planning to go to the state she lived in. On several occasions I had tried to meet her, only to my disappointment. I had a deep feeling I was supposed to go there, but I knew Gene didn't feel that he should take me due to her inhospitable attitude over the years. We continued to pray for her through all the years, but her heart was hard because of her son not doing things her way. Gene told me he would take me to see her when he heard she was in the hospital, if he knew God wanted him to. I knew I needed a miracle for it to happen.

Well, his brother decided to go there and one miracle after another took place during his stay there. He is a Colonel in the Army, and the older brother. He ended up calling Gene and telling me to come with Gene to Colorado so we could all meet to pray together. He saw that her physical weakness was softening her heart... it was the miracle I was waiting for. He had prayed with one of the nurses and called and said he felt like we were all to gather and pray together for their mother. We left the next day.

I knew in my heart we might be staying there for a period of time, and I went to meet the "stranger" I had loved through the years, with no response. Her son was a blessing sent from heaven for me and others and I so wanted to be able to tell her how he had fulfilled God's promises in the Scripture, Acts 13:47, "I have set thee to be a light of the Gentiles, that thou shouldest be for salvation unto the ends of the earth." I so wanted to share the fact that God's Son Jesus has power to change lives and He sends men into His field of labor to do His work. I cried when the opportunity was presented me in reality to thank her for the son she bore. She ended up seeing her son was a blessing sent from God to her, too, in the end!

Apprehensive, I prayed and decided to put on love for one who had shown me nothing but rejection. Jesus strengthened me. She was a bit cold to me and Gene at first, but the first day there, she let me take her to the bathroom. I knew the greatest weapon God had given me to use on her was love, so I poured it on! IT WORKED TOO!

I think she had been offended with Gene throughout the years for letting go of helping in the family business. Both of her sons had moved on, and she had been overcome by the bottle. I could tell she was very perceptive in evaluating how selfish people are! Many times people can see into others, even things they fail to look at in themselves. I knew she was no dumb cookie! She had the ability to see what people were made of and her piercing eyes were checking me out to see what I was made of!

She was weak and let us bring her strength through praying with her. One week after I was caring for her she looked at me and said, "God bless you; I love you Ceci." I thought I was hearing her wrong; I went back in the room and asked her if she knew who I was. She replied and said, "Yes, you're Gene's wife, Ceci." I went in the other room and cried my eyes out. I knew God's love had reached her.

We treated her like a queen. We did everything we could to bring her life pleasure, because it was obvious that her days on the earth were numbered. Our friend Linda came to help us. I began talking to her about her depression. I think she talked more to us than she had talked to anyone about how she really felt in years. She began asking us to stay in her room and keep her company. One night she even asked Linda to pray for her, and of course that is exactly what we were hoping and praying for; we were all in tears.

She was finally reaching out to the One who could really comfort her, the Lover of her soul, the God who created her. I asked her if she wanted me to redecorate her room, and a joy for living came into her heart. She began to experience the JOY OF LOVING AND BEING LOVED! We rented all her favorite old movies, and got her favorite foods. She hadn't been eating well for a while, but her appetite even returned.

One morning I went in her room to have her say, "How can you take care of me like this? I don't understand how you cannot be having all kinds of bitter, critical thoughts towards taking care of me. It's got to be really rough on you to care for me." I told her that serving sin and living in the hell that I had lived in by LOVING MYSELF ABOVE ALL THINGS, is what was really hard. I told her about the time I broke down crying because I realized God had given me something greater to live for than my own little happy life... which was in misery. I was so thankful to think I didn't have to go out of this world only caring for my selfish little desires.

I was so happy He had called me to a greater purpose, FOR THE SAVING AND KEEPING OF SOULS! "Taking care of you," I said, "is a piece of cake and I never had a bad attitude." LIVING TO LOVE HER WAS HEAVEN ON EARTH ABOVE LIVING TO LOVE MYSELF! I said that she was the only one having a bad attitude and that was not coming from me, but from the king of bad attitudes... the king of darkness. She would say at times... "I'll be damned," and I told her, "no you won't; that's why Jesus sent us, so you wouldn't be damned." I told her she was fortunate to have two praying sons, because she could be in hell on earth in a nursing home!

Gene went in her room one morning and said, "The Lord told me He spoke to you when you were about to crash in the forest in your new plane." The snow was very deep; she was headed for the trees in her new plane. She heard the words, "I'm going to get you out of this Pattie." Gene asked her if it was true and she said "Yes." Gene said, "The Lord told me to tell you He's going to get you out of this one, too! All you have to do is ask Him, and He'll take you from this world into His kingdom when it's your time to go on." Gene cried as he spoke to her and you could see she was deeply moved to tears herself in knowing God was using her son to speak words to her about her past that ONLY GOD KNEW.

She had lived with the television on before we got there; but now she wanted it off for the most part, because she was experiencing the PEACE OF GOD WHICH PASSES ALL UNDERSTANDING FOR THE FIRST TIME IN HER LIFE. That was something very unusual. We played Christian music often and that was very different for her. She really had joy and peace from it, and told us it made her feel good. On her birthday, I finished redecorating her room. She was so pleased with the new colors and spirit, but little did we know what a short time she had to enjoy it. We did not even realize the cake and ice cream she was eating would be her last meal. She had come down with a cold and she didn't have the strength to fight it.

Three days later, Gene's mom went on to glory and to see Jesus face to face! We thought her cold may have been a blessing in disguise that kept her from long months of suffering. As Gene's brother put it, "She was one more soul snatched free from the clutches of Satan, and the kingdom of darkness!" I think I'm still in shock over seeing an 81-year old turn from darkness into the Kingdom of Light. Actually, Linda's father had repented of his dark, little selfish world too, in his old age. He decided to go out of this life receiving and giving love, too, rather than dying a bitter, critical man.

Surely Pat was a worker in the vineyard in the last minutes of her life of three weeks. We saw the parable fulfilled where Jesus paid the same wage to the ones who worked all day, and the one who worked the last minute! She found His mercy and experienced His lovingkindness and found relief for her heavy burdens these last three weeks of her life. We will never forget God's faithfulness to help us reach her soul while we were in her home; now she gets to be in HIS HOME! She went from being demonized (which means to be energized by the wrong spirit). It's like running your car on bad gas — that bitter, critical, selfish gas. She turned, repented, and put the gas of love and faith in her heart, and went from being a sick, sin-laden soul, to a giver and receiver of His love.

Jesus said in Matthew 10:40: "He that receiveth you receiveth me, and he that receiveth me receiveth him that sent me." He also said in Matthew 25:37-40: "Then shall the righteous answer him, saying, Lord, when saw we thee an hungred, and fed thee? or thirsty, and gave thee drink? When saw we thee a stranger, and took thee in? or naked, and clothed thee? Or when saw we thee sick, or in prison, and came unto thee? And the King shall answer and say unto them, Verily I say unto you, Inasmuch as ye have done it unto one of the least of these my brethren, ye have done it unto me." The love of God in our hearts is a rich treasure we have to spend. May we all die with no savings in our love bank!

It's so exciting to see the goodness of God —which can lead one to repentance — work in the last three weeks of her life! His wonders never cease to amaze us! We experienced the Glory of God as she slipped out of this world and into His Kingdom today! We all cried as we sat around after she was gone and marveled at the wondrous things that had taken place! We were filled with rejoicing for her, but sorrow for us... as we came to know a very sweet and precious woman — one who spent 81 years as a mean, intimidating, depressed, destructive and hard-hearted woman. It was a great joy to give her the love of Jesus, and to receive her love! (She decided to let it out instead of being a withholder.)

This definitely is a time in my life I will never forget! And I'm filled with joy to know there is another jewel in the crown of my Savior! I told her to tell Jesus we love Him when she sees Him face to face... even as she's in His presence this day!

CHAPTER 28

Jesus Power
The Mary Faber Story

I was raised in a Christian Reformed church atmosphere, and my father was an elder of the church where we attended. I felt very indifferent in that environment, except for when I became involved with a group within the church called S.W.I.M. (Summer Workshop in Missions). Also, at the age of twelve I fell out of a car with epilepsy resulting, which is in mild form now.

Circumstances led me to where I left the church after losing my ex-husband and son in one month's time, which was through a very painful divorce. I began to hang around with the wrong people, and the next thing I knew, I realized I was in a gang (Latin Manic Disciples). When I realized I was in a gang, I felt hurt and hostile, wondering why Jesus was allowing all these things to happen to me. After all, I was an elder's daughter and was active in the church. Later I felt Jesus rejected me, but I realize now that it was me who rejected Him. The things I did were like dead works, but yet Jesus kept His arms outstretched to me. You see, I only served Him half-heartedly, as I look back on it now.

One day when I was in the gang, I decided *enough is enough.* I was never brought up this way, and everything they did was wrong. It wasn't Jesus' way and I knew better. I had just finished praying to Jesus as the guys came back. They asked me if I had been praying, and I told them, "Of course I was," and everything came out about what was going on inside of me. They realized that I had just given my life to Jesus Christ.

I should be six feet under, but Jesus saved me from the jaws of death. The next night after I had prayed and asked Jesus to come into my heart, I had a guy who I used to go out with, try to kill me with a knife. He couldn't do it, so his twin brother tried to kill me two weeks later. I had been sleeping when I felt something touching me; I woke up seeing him (the twin) standing over me with a knife in his hand.

When he tried to plunge the knife into my body, he couldn't because it was as if someone was holding his arm. Every time he tried, the knife went into his hand instead. All I could see were beautiful feet and a pure whitish-blue gown, which was raised in the air. Then I looked at the other guys in the room and they looked so *very scared.* I thought it must have been one of Jesus' angels there preventing this man from killing me, and then the vision of beautiful feet and the pure whitish-blue gown disappeared.

All I could hear was a windy sound and one of the guys saying, "Don't you have any respect for God?" The next morning I asked the twin brother about his hand just to see what he would say. He said the cuts on his hand happened at work and for me to get away from him. I went into the bathroom and just laughed and thanked God for sparing my life!

Then two days later, they lied to me again and told me a girlfriend was going to meet me there. But they thought it was just another way to get rid of me once and for all. They held a gun to the temple of my head, which made me *very* angry! I said Jesus' Name under my breath. They told me "God can't help you now!" That made me even more hostile toward what they wanted to do. When they tried shooting the gun, it only clicked. I had just recently put a new bullet in that gun, and the next thing I knew they were blaming each other for the gun not working right. They just told me to get out of there, so I ran to a school across the street and hid in the bushes for awhile, and then left when I felt it was safe again.

Jesus doesn't make all of your problems go away, but He will always be there when you need Him. You just need to call on His Name; He is listening no matter what you are doing or where you are. If it is family problems, marital problems, financial problems or whatever, Jesus has a miracle with your name on it! Whatever is bothering you at anytime in your life, even if it is a bad report from the doctor, Jesus can help. He loves you so much!

He was born in a stable, walked this earth, did many miracles, healed many people and was just a carpenter's son. Most importantly, He was the Son of God and He died for you and for me, was buried, arose from the grave, and is coming back for us again. When He comes back are we going to be ready? Will Jesus be in your heart? Will you be working *for* Jesus instead of *against* Him?

Since Jesus came into my heart, I have been writing a book about how He saved my life: how he saved me, healed me, and set me on fire for Him. I have a real purpose in life; I thought I had purpose before I knew Jesus personally, but knowing Him personally gives me such a high I had never experienced before. I'm happy all of the time and I don't have to put money on a store counter to get cigarettes or alcohol anymore. Jesus made you and He loves you!

Heaven is for Jesus and His angels and all those who make Him Savior and Lord of their lives, but hell was made for only Satan and his demons. Don't be in chains when you can have real freedom. Don't wait to have Jesus come into your heart; you must ask Him to come in. What if you get in an accident or die while sleeping, and you haven't yet asked Jesus to come into your heart and life? When you die, people at your funeral will say, "It's too bad; he or she wanted to give their life to Jesus Christ before they died, but now it's too late." Please don't let that be what happens to you!

If you would like to ask Jesus Christ to come into your life, please say this prayer sincerely from your heart and He will hear you and meet you at your point of need in your life:

Dear Heavenly Father, I know I am a sinner and need Your forgiveness. I repent of my sins. I believe that You sent Your Son Jesus Christ who died for my sins; He was raised from the dead, and sits on the right hand of God Almighty. I turn from my sins and invite Jesus Christ to come into my heart and life. Thank you, Lord, for saving my soul! In Jesus' Name, I pray this. Amen.

If you just prayed that prayer, welcome to the family of God! My gentle Savior will lead you day by day. Please don't hide what you've just done — go and tell someone! Let your light shine before men and Him!

"Ye are the light of the world. A city that is set on an hill cannot be hid. Neither do men light a candle, and put it under a bushel, but on a candlestick; and it giveth light unto all that are in the house. Let your light so shine before men, that they may see your good works, and glorify your Father which is in heaven." (Matthew 5:14-16).

Thank you and God bless you for letting me share what Jesus means to me. I pray that you will continue to grow in His grace and love in your life!

Kind permission was given by Precious Testimonies to share this testimony.

CHAPTER 29

The Love We Shared Keeps Touching Others
As told by Seeloy DuBois

It was Saturday, 27 August 2005. That day I was celebrating my birthday of 29 years. Usually my mother would call at the break of dawn to wish me well, but that day I slept in late. The phone finally rang but it was not the call I was expecting. It was my sister Kim. She resides in Canada. For a split second I was happy. The thought of her remembering my birthday made my day. To my surprise, her voice just wasn't the same. I asked her what the matter was. She told me her mother-in-law had passed away that Thursday and today was the funeral. She then went on to say, "Daddy is really sick. No one knows what's wrong, except he has a high temperature and he is really weak."

She had just spoken to Mom and they were trying to decide where to take him. My parents live in Trinidad. That's in the Caribbean. The emergency system there is really not for emergencies. I told my sister I was going to call Mommy to find out what's really going on. That's when Kim said something that really disturbed me. She said "Please pray for him." She went on to say she was worried because death comes in double. I immediately told her I do not believe in that superstition. With that I hung up and dialed what used to be my old home number.

The phone rang twice and then my mother answered. She was concerned for her husband of 35 years. I asked her for an update. She stated that Daddy had an abscess in his buttock, he had a high temperature and he was very weak because he had not eaten the past three days. Then in the background I heard him ask who was on the phone. She called out my name, and then passed the phone over to him.

When Dad came on the phone, we were both silent. Then with no warning he started to cry. I tried comforting him, but for some reason the right words could not come out of my mouth. I wanted to tell him I loved him and everything would be okay. The words 'I love you, Dad,' could not come out. I have never heard my father say those words to me or any one else for that matter. I say it to my husband and my kids but I could not find it in me to say it to him. He knew I loved him and I knew he felt the same. It was understood . . . but never said out loud.

I asked him why he waited until he was so sick before saying something to Mom. Then I said with a stern voice, yet still crying, "Daddy, you will get through this; and when you do you will have to change your life — stop smoking, start praying, altogether change your life." I said all I could, then he murmured to me, "Okay."

When my mother came on the phone she wanted to know what I told him that would make him cry like that. I gave her the short version of what happened, and then she said my sister Keisha had arrived to take him to a private hospital. We said goodbye, and I was told as soon as they checked in, they would give me a call with an update.

When I hung up the phone, I could not stop crying. I was mad that my sister mentioned that death comes in double. I wanted to be there for my dad. It was too much to bear so I did the best thing I know how and that was to pray. I told my husband what was going on and he, too, dropped on his knees.

So far my birthday had started out a little rough, but it got better. My family presented me with my presents and they told me how much they loved me. That brought a smile back to my face. I started to cook a big lunch because I was on my way to celebrate my birthday with fellow choir members at a friend's house.

About three hours later, while I was in the kitchen, the phone rang. It was my other sister Amoy. She was on her way to the hospital to see Daddy but took the time to call and gave me the number to my sister Keisha's cell, so I could call right away. She told me they were going to do the surgery to drain the abscess and the family wanted me to talk to him before he went in. I called the cell number and sure enough Keisha answered; then within a second I was on with Dad again. I asked him how he was doing and he whimpered, "Not well." I told him not to worry. I assured him that after the surgery he would feel a lot better and that I was praying for him.

Then we were back to that moment again. I got the urge to say, 'I love you, Dad,' but could not. I was silent for a few seconds, then I gathered my thoughts and said I would call him when I got back home from my birthday party. Keisha took the phone and felt really bad for not remembering, and so did my mom. But that was the least of our thoughts, even for me.

We had a nice time at the party. While I was there I couldn't help thinking about how my day started. No one else knew what happened that day except a handful of people I spoke to. I could not wait to get home to call my mom to get an update. When we walked in the house, I made sure the kids were ready for bed before I called, because I did not want to be disturbed. Before I knew it, the phone rang. It was Kim. The first thing she said to me was not to worry. Of course, that's exactly what I did. She started out by saying, "He will be okay." I was not in the mood for games. I blurted out: "Just tell me what's going on!" Then she started spilling out everything. "The doctors did not operate. Daddy had a heart attack." I almost passed out. She told me not to cry, but just pray. I told her I wanted to call Keisha and find out what the real story was.

I dialed the number as fast as I could. After one ring she picked up. As soon as she heard my voice she started to sniffle as if holding back tears. I told her what I heard and wanted details. She said, "Daddy did not know he was having a heart attack. It was a really small one. It was only detected by the monitor. The reason for not operating was due to the fact he was too weak because of not eating for days, and the abscess was so infected they could not put him under anesthetic until he was stronger." She went on to say that she had good news. I was thinking... *anything after today must be good news.* Earlier that night she told her husband Darryl to go into the room and pray for Daddy. He agreed and they both stood by his bedside and prayed for him.

After the "Amen," Darryl left the room and she decided to stay and chat for a while. She asked him why did he do this to himself. Why didn't he call her if he was feeling ill, or someone else, for that matter. He told her he was used to breaking out in boils about his skin and he thought this one was just another. The reason for not eating was a result of being in too much pain to go to the bathroom. He came to the conclusion that if he did not eat he would not pass stool and that would eliminate him having more pain than he could handle. Then he told her he had not slept for four days. She asked him "Why? Were you in so much pain you could not sleep?"

That's when he said the unthinkable. He said, "When I close my eyes, I see these ugly-looking things at the foot of my bed."

Keisha was startled. She asked, "What do you *mean*, ugly-looking things? Do you mean demons?!" He shook his head in confirmation.

Keisha stood up, full of conviction, dropped to her knees and started to pray, rebuking the demons away. She said while she was praying, he was calling out to her in a frantic voice, but she did not stop. She kept on going. Within a few moments he stopped calling out to her and in a calm tone he told her they were leaving the bedside. She continued for a few more seconds.

Then she told him if he ever saw them again, repeat these words "I rebuke you in the NAME OF JESUS!" He shook his head in agreement. Without further delay the Holy Spirit took over and He prompted Keisha to ask Dad, "Do you love Jesus?" Without hesitation he said, "Yes. I love Him very much."

I think that was the first time anyone of us had ever heard Dad say he loved *anyone.* Then like clockwork she asked him if he ever said the sinner's prayer. He said he had, a long time ago when he was a little boy. He told her he lived with a lady who would take care of him and she took him to church. He never kept up with it. Funny, I always thought my dad grew up with his mother. I guess for some time he was under the care of someone else.

At that very moment he said he wanted to say it again. "He was very anxious," Keisha said. The Holy Spirit gave her the words to say and Daddy repeated word for word. When they were finished, he told her he was really sleepy, and to see to it that no one came by to visit him. He did not want to be disturbed. In no time at all he was snoring. He was sound asleep. After all, he had to catch up on four days of lost sleep.

When all was said, I felt a warm, comforting feeling. I felt as if I had won the lottery. In a way it was. The grand prize was eternal life for my father. Even though he was still really sick, and we had no idea what was wrong, we knew no matter what the eventual outcome would be okay. I will never forget that day for the rest of my life. The day I was born, on 27 August, my father was spiritually born again. That night I prayed and praised God for what His Son Jesus did for my dad. I had a restful sleep knowing he was going to be okay.

The next day was Sunday. What a day for rejoicing and praise. I was walking around as if I was on air. We got up and got dressed for church as usual. Before I left the house I called my dad and told him I was on my way to church and that I was happy with the decision he made last evening. I told him I would pray for him and I would call him when I got back. He sounded better, a little stronger than before.

When we got in church, the pastor's wife Ruthie greeted me. She immediately asked how my dad was doing. I said, "Great!" I briefly told her he was still very sick but he had given his life to Christ last night. She was overjoyed.

I joined the rest of the choir on stage and not long after we started to sing. The song we sang was "God is Still Doing Great Things." I could not get the words to come out of my mouth. I was so emotional; I was crying yet I wanted to burst out laughing. It was a feeling I cannot explain. I had no other choice but to share my dad's testimony to my church. When the song was finished, I walked over to Ruthie and told her I had a confession. She corrected me, and said, "You mean *testimony*." That was the enemy trying to confuse me. She then waved at her husband, who then gave me the microphone.

My dad's testimony went throughout the entire church. People were crying, then laughing, then praising God. God is still doing great things. After the service, a lot of people came up to me and thanked me for sharing. They said that after hearing the testimony, their hope had been renewed for *their* dads and relatives. I was glad I was able to share. I could not keep that inside.

We then drove over to my aunt and uncle's house for Sunday lunch. Not long after we ate, the phone rang and it was my sister Keisha. We spoke for a short while then Dad came on. He sounded weaker than before. I gave the phone to Aunty, so she could say "Hi." I saw the look on her face change. I asked, "What happened?" She said, "He started crying again." She gave me the phone and Keisha came back to say, "Keep praying. The surgery is tomorrow."

That night, when we got home, I prayed for a good night's rest for my family and healing for my dad. The next morning, I was getting dressed for work. I made a quick call to my dad, asking him what time was the surgery. He said he was not sure. I told him, "I will call you tonight when I get back."

Later that day my husband called my office and told me he got a call from Trinidad. The surgery went well and Dad was resting. I couldn't wait to get home to call.

As soon as I got there I called for a little more detail. Mom answered and sounded a lot better than the last time I spoke to her. She said my sister Kim was coming in from Canada that Wednesday. Dad was doing a lot better. "The pain is almost gone." He was under a lot of antibiotics and painkillers. That accounted for him having no more pain, but at least he was comfortable. Mom said she told the doctors to do a full body exam and let us know what the cause of his condition is. My father hated being in the hospital and now that he was there she wanted to take full advantage of the situation.

The doctors told her that by Wednesday, 31 August, they would be able to run some tests and know for sure what was going on in his body. The next few days were almost routine. I called every morning before I went to work, and the moment I walked back in the house, I needed my progress report.

That Wednesday night my family and I were on our way to vacation. We would be gone for a total of six days. I called my dad like I would always do and spoke to him about my day and asked him about his. I told him I would not be able to call him until I got back. I told him what my plans were and without even giving it another thought I said, "I love you." He replied "Me, too." I thought to myself...*This is good enough.* I felt so relieved to know I said it. I felt like a burden was lifted off of me. I went on my vacation feeling happy, satisfied, relieved, loved and comforted.

We had a great time. Even though we were having the time of our lives, I was more anxious to get home to get an update on my father. I had a great time sharing my dad's testimony with the relatives we were with. On 6 September, we were awakened by a call on my husband's cell phone. The signal was very poor so he went outside the building to continue his call. I got up right away with the thought of going home to call my dad. I got the kids up and served their breakfast, then went back to my room to have a little peace and quiet while I ate. All that time went by and my husband was nowhere to be found. I did not really look for him because I was busy with the kids, but something in me knew something was not right.

As soon as he walked in the door of our room, I asked him who called. He told me it was my uncle Joe. I was surprised but yet not. He asked me if I had a nice time here and asked if I was okay. I answered his questions but wanted answers for mine. "*Why* did he call?" My husband took a deep breath and said, "He called about your dad. It is critical." I looked at him with a confused look on my face. The first thought that came to mind was *how could he be critical?* When I spoke to him last he was doing better.

Then the bomb dropped. "Your dad died this morning." I felt my heart jump out of my body and fall flat on the ground and break into a million pieces. A tidal wave of tears rushed to my eyes. The next thing I felt was pure confusion. I forgot where I was, who I was with, and lost all sense of mental control. Those words rang through my head like a broken record. I had to get out! At some point I forgot to breathe. I felt the walls closing in on me. I had to get out. I got loose from my husband's grip and took off running. I ran outside to the pool. I needed the fresh air. Someone told me they were sorry and gave me a hug on my way out, but I felt nothing.

I walked around the pool trying to get clarity on the whole situation. I couldn't. I just could not imagine my life without my dad. This was impossible. I sat down for a second and felt my husband's arm around me. I needed answers; I needed details. I wanted to know exactly how it happened and why. I asked my husband to tell me what happened. He did not have any answers. He called my uncle Joe. Joe said, "Mom was looking for Dad in the bedroom but he was not there. She then checked the bathroom and found him on the floor."

I needed the truth but could not handle the truth. People all around were telling me he was with Jesus. But I wanted him here with me. The phone rang again. It was a friend from church. He gave me words of comfort. He said the right things, but nothing made a difference. Here I was crying my eyes out, my children were crying wanting to know what was wrong, my husband trying to be strong for me, comforting me, holding me and doing the best he could.

The next call I got was from my mother. The first thing she said to me was not to worry. I was sick and tired of people telling me not to worry. I wanted the truth. She took a deep breath and told me the story. The Friday after I left on my vacation, the doctors came in the room with the results of the tests. They told my mother, "Your husband is sicker than you think. When he fully recovers from the operation, he will have to start taking dialysis. His kidneys are 100% not working, and the abscess was a result of the infection in his blood."

She said, "Your father wanted to return home on Friday but he was instructed to stay. A lot of relatives came to visit him in the hospital and some called from overseas. By Monday he was begging to come home. He convinced everyone if he was released from the hospital he would be more rested and eat more food. He stated he hated hospital food and wanted my home cooking. The doctors sent him home as he requested. He was taken to Keisha's house. She lived one block from the hospital. He was happy to be away from the hospital. However, Monday night he was sitting on the porch and he was daydreaming, and then came back to reality."

Mom continued, "He had the same look his mother had the day she passed and went to be with the Lord. That night, he went to bed and lay across sideways, not allowing any room for her to sleep. I told him to roll over and make room for me. He told me I did not have to sleep with him. He insisted he was okay."

"The next morning when I got up early to check on him and make a cup of tea, when I got to the bedroom, he was not on the bed. I then walked towards the bathroom and there he was lying on the floor. I hugged him and he was still warm. I called out for help. When the ambulance came they announced he was dead."

That's how it happened. I wanted the truth and got it. After hearing what happened and having that mental picture played over and over in my mind, I felt that feeling of joy starting to bubble up inside of me once again. My sadness over-powered that joy. That's when it happened. I felt someone hug me, but there was no one around. Then as clear as bell, I heard these words, *"He is with Me."*

The joy that was bubbling started to boil over. I felt this warm feeling inside of me. I was crying, but deep down inside I knew he was okay. My next move was to try to find a way to go back to Trinidad. I was not prepared for this; we did not have enough resources to travel. I refused to go without my husband. Dad had died that Tuesday and the funeral was to be on Friday, 9 September. I told Mom I would try to come. That's when her voice changed and she sounded like a mother again.

She said the family had a meeting and decided it was best that I did not come to the funeral. She also mentioned my father told her if anything ever happened to him, "Tell Seeloy not to come." She said it was his wishes. He knew the price for the tickets would be too much to handle, and he wanted my family and I to visit at a happier time. She insisted I save the money and use it for a happier time. I was upset the family had made this decision for me, but it's the last thing I could do and respect his wishes. That day we made the decision not to go. It was killing me inside but I had to obey. The family updated me in everything that took place in preparation for the funeral. I was told to e-mail a letter so my uncle Boyo would read it on my behalf at the funeral. It took me almost one hour to write that letter. Finally I got to the end.

The next day I got a call from my sister, saying they got the letter and it was beautiful. There were hundreds of people at the house every night from the day he died until the funeral. Mom said everyone was really nice to her and she had a lot of help. The Lord was blessing my family. Strangers came up to my sisters and told them how much my father meant to them and how much he was there for them when they needed him. We were so proud hearing these things.

Friday, 9 September: the day of the funeral was here. I just wanted to be alone. Every day got a little better but not fast enough. Around 12:00 p.m. my mother called and said the body had arrived at the house. I asked her what was he wearing. She described him with compassion and love. "He wore a pair of black pants, a white shirt with a black bow tie and his favorite red hat." She said, "He looks 30 years younger." Amoy came on the phone and said, "He looks like he is on a beach somewhere." That was comforting. Then Mom said to me, "The family decided that *you* should read the letter yourself." I was confused. I did not know what was going on, but I went along with it. My brother came on the phone and said I would get a call around 2:30 and I was to be ready to read the letter. I agreed, and then hung up.

The time dragged on that day. Two hours felt like ten. When the hour drew near, I locked myself in the room and waited for the call. Sure enough, the call came on time. Someone was singing and my brother told me to wait until he was finished. When the music stopped I heard the pastor say, "We have a letter from Seeloy from the United States." That was my cue. I poured my heart out. This is what I wrote:

Dear Daddy,

Even though you are gone, I have such great memories of moments we shared together. These are a few of my favorites.

I remember waking up before sunrise and coming out to the living room and watching you drink your morning coffee while standing at the front door. You would look back at me and give me your cup ... with just enough for a mouthful. Even though I did not like the taste of coffee, I drank it because you gave it to me. That was you telling me you loved me.

After dinner time you would give me your plate to take to the kitchen and you would leave just a mouthful of chicken for me. That was you telling me you loved me.

When I told you I was getting married and you were so happy you could not stop smiling. That was you telling me you loved me.

On my wedding day, when we were on our way to the church, you were crying your eyes out. Although you made me cry and mess up my make-up on my big day, I knew then how much you loved me.

Daddy, I never heard you say the words "I love you," but deep in my heart I knew you did.

When I would sit and scratch your head for an hour, that was me telling you "I love you."

When I would bring home Chinese food for you after work, that was me telling you "I love you."

When I slipped you a twenty every now and again, that was me telling you "I love you."

Even though we could not say it to each other, there is no mistake about it. You loved me and I loved you.

When I got that call from Trinidad saying you were really ill, I called you right away to tell you I loved you, but I couldn't. I told you I missed you but could not say the words "I love you."

Later that night when Keisha called and said you gave your life to Christ and that you love Jesus, I felt this overwhelming joy take over my heart. I knew at that moment no matter what the outcome, I will see you again, whether it is here on earth or later in heaven.

On 31 August, 2005 at 7:46 p.m., I called you and we spoke for awhile. I told you I was going out of town on vacation and that I would call back on 6 September, when I returned. After a few laughs, my last words to you were "I love you."

Daddy, I love you... I love you... I love you...I love you...

I am sorry I did not say it enough, but when I see you again, it will be playing in your head like a broken record that could never be turned off.

The news of you passing broke my heart into a million pieces. Everyone tried comforting me but nothing anyone said to me made a difference.

Then the Holy Sprit came in and comforted me. He gave me a big hug and whispered in my ear that you are with Jesus. He said, "The pain you were feeling here on earth is no more," and then He left me with these words: "I LOVE YOU."

This is not goodbye, but see you later...

With lots and lots of love,

Your daughter,
Seeloy DuBois

CONCLUSION

This book shared important testimonies from the lives of some courageous people who made life-changing decisions. Their decisions changed their eternal destinies. If there is any doubt as to your eternal destiny or salvation, then today, I urge you to consider the following Scriptures.

"As it is written, There is none righteous, no, not one." (Romans 3:10).

"For all have sinned, and come short of the glory of God." (Romans 3:23).

"For the wages of sin is death; but the gift of God is eternal life through Jesus Christ our Lord." (Romans 6:23).

"For there is one God, and one mediator between God and men, the man Christ Jesus." (1 Timothy 2:5).

"That if thou shalt confess with thy mouth the Lord Jesus, and shalt believe in thine heart that God hath raised him from the dead, thou shalt be saved. For with the heart man believeth unto righteousness; and with the mouth confession is made unto salvation." (Romans 10:9-10).

Now, here is a Sinner's Prayer to receive Jesus as Lord and Savior. Please repeat the following prayer and mean it from your heart:

"Dear Heavenly Father, I come to You in the Name of the Lord Jesus Christ. I ask You to forgive me of all my sins. I accept Jesus as my Lord and Savior and believe in my heart that He died on the cross for my sins, and that You raised Him from the dead so that I could be in right standing with You. I now repent and confess Jesus as my Lord and Savior. I thank You for giving me eternal salvation and ask that You would help me in my Christian walk."

I strongly encourage you to read your Bible daily to get to know the Lord better, talk to God daily in prayer and find a church where the Bible is taught as the complete Word of God.

COMPILED BY

Commander Michael H. Imhof, U.S. Navy (retired), was born in Fort Bragg, North Carolina and raised in Blasdell, New York. He attended the State University College of New York at Buffalo, where he received a Bachelor of Science degree. He was commissioned in 1973. After completing Basic Underwater Demolition/SEAL training in Coronado, California, Commander Imhof was assigned to SEAL Team TWO, and subsequent Naval Special Warfare and other type commands.

Commander Imhof, possessing a Naval Special Warfare designator, has served throughout the world in numerous positions. Assignments include Platoon Commander, Training Officer, Operations Officer, Staff Officer, Executive Officer and Commanding Officer. He also earned a Master's Degree in Administration from George Washington University and served as an instructor at the U.S. Naval Academy. His awards include Defense Meritorious Service Medal; Meritorious Service Medal with two Gold Stars in lieu of second and third awards; Joint Service Commendation Medal; Navy Commendation Medal with Gold Star in lieu of second award; United Nations Medal; and other service awards. Commander Imhof also worked in Afghanistan in support of the Department of State after his military career.

A military officer of strong Christian convictions, Commander Imhof is ready and willing to share his faith with all. He is convinced that the Bible is the authoritative and uncompromised Word of God and gives thanks for the wonderful blessings of God in his life and the lives of his family. He is an active member in his local church.

Previous books include *Lessons From Bible Characters*, *More Lessons From Bible Characters*, and *Walking With God* (*A Daily Devotional of Spiritual Truths in Poetic Form*), and *Testimonies of Ex-Muslims*.

To Order Additional Copies of this Book Please Contact:

Evangel Press
2000 Evangel Way
Nappanee, IN 46550
1-800-253-9315
www.evangelpress.com